ARCHITECTURAL PHILOSOPHY

ARCHITECTURAL PHILOSOPHY

ANDREW BENJAMIN

THE ATHLONE PRESS
LONDON & NEW BRUNSWICK, NJ

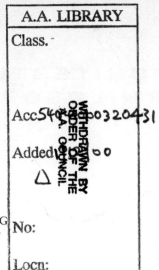
First published in 2000 by
THE ATHLONE PRESS
1 Park Drive, London NW11 7SG
and New Brunswick, New Jersey

British Library Cataloguing in Publication Data
A catalogue record for this book is available from the British Library

ISBN 0 485 00415 1 (HB)
ISBN 0 485 00605 7 (PB)

Library of Congress Cataloging-in-Publication Data
Benjamin, Andrew E.
    Architectural philosophy : repetition, function, alterity/
    Andrew Benjamin.
        p.   cm.
    Includes bibliographical references and index.
    ISBN 0–485–00415–1 (case: alk. paper)
    ISBN 0–485–00605–7 (pbk: alk. paper)
    I. Title.
NA2500.B463 2000-06-20
720'.1   dc21   00–038944

Distributed in The United States, Canada and South America by
Transaction Publishers
390 Campus Drive
Somerset, New Jersey 08873

Typeset by Florence Production Ltd, Stoodleigh, Devon
Printed and bound in Great Britain by
Bookcraft (Bath) Ltd

CONTENTS

PREFACE

This book is the result of trying to think through the relationship between architecture and philosophy. Teaching in the Graduate School of Architecture Planning and Preservation at Columbia University and more recently at the Architectural Association in London coupled to teaching the occasional undergraduate courses in aesthetics in the Department of Philosophy at the University of Warwick in which architecture figured, I have had the opportunity to work with outstanding colleagues and students in remarkable and exacting institutions.[1] The project was always presented as teaching philosophy to architecture students or architectural concerns to students of philosophy. And yet it was never that simple. For both sets of students, though equally for colleagues involved in all these institutions, the question of relation proved the most demanding. That there is a relationship goes without saying. That philosophy uses architectural metaphors is clearly the case. That architecture deploys a language that is in part philosophical is also now commonplace. That in the founding texts of architectural theory – e.g. Vitruvius, Alberti – there are passages and insights that would be equally at home in philosophical texts concerning aesthetics, is both well known and yet not remarkable.

The question of the relation between philosophy and architecture is both already staged and yet to be addressed in a way that allows for the particularity of the architectural to be maintained. Philosophy has a tendency of reducing the visual arts and architecture to a body of examples. Works are deployed as evidence for a particular argument or as an example of a more generalized movement. The question to which this book can be taken as a response is the following : What happens when the reductive move is refused and the constraint is having to think the particularity of the architectural? Once this question is posed then a range of other questions follow. All of them are concerned with the philosophical or theoretical problem of addressing particularity.

There is already a response to the insistence of the particular. Simple empirical description is a way both of addressing specificity and allowing for the detail of architecture. Leaving aside the question of whether or not description is itself already a theoretical position, there is still the problem that the generality of the description will fail to engage with architecture understood as a site of repetition. What is repeated is that which is given in order to be repeated. Much of the work of this book is an attempt to link the specificity of architecture to a conception of function. Rather than taking function as a given it is rearticulated within a structure of repetition. While a concern with particularity will always involve recourse to the detail of the particular that detail is not on its own sufficient.

The chapters comprising this book have been written over the last few years.[2] They represent an attempt to develop a project. It was too easy to plot the relationship between architecture and philosophy in terms of a shared language. There is a very real sense in which operating at the level of metaphor – both as a way of proceeding and as a site of investigation – fails to address either the particularity of the architectural or the philosophical. In attempting to move from an analysis taking place on the level of language to another level there seemed to be the need to develop certain concepts in order to effect that move. Part of what is presented here needs to be read in that light. In other words, rather than treat architecture and philosophy as though they were both texts in which there was either an overlap or similarity of language such that an analysis of the language was an analysis of the relation, there is an approach which takes the demands of architectural work as that which necessitates a response that pertains to philosophy or the theoretical.

The question – what is the thinking of architecture? – has to begin with a thinking of architecture. On one level this is a tautology. On another it is not. It is the latter precisely because the means for thinking architecture – not architecture as language, or as sign system or as the domain of examples – have not been developed in a sustained way. The chapters making up this book can be read as continual attempts to develop such a thinking. As such they comprise architectural philosophy.

PART I

COMPLEX SPACING

INTRODUCTION

Guiding the analysis of architectural works by Peter Eisenman and Reiser and Umemoto is a specific commitment. While it takes different forms the overall claim is that the possibility of experimentation and therefore the possibility of alterity and criticality within architecture, depends upon retaining particularity as the site of activity. Particularity in architecture is indissolubly connected to function. What this means is that the locus of the critical and thus the domain of experimentation are ultimately linked to creating other possibilities within and for function. This is not the reiteration of the claim that forms follows function. On the contrary, there is no need why a given particular should have an already determined form. (That it does is a separate and important historical and theoretical question.) Rather, the claim is that once an object – be it a diagram, plan or building – is assumed to be architectural then the interpretive question concerns how that object works as architecture.[1] Any answer to that question is necessarily constrained by the presence of function. The project of Chapter 1 is to pursue some of the detail of this claim. Function cannot be simply posited. There needs to a theoretical account of how the presence of function is to be understood. This is made all the more urgent by the related claim that function is the ineliminable element within the architectural.

Function, it will be argued, cannot be thought outside a complex structure of repetition. Function is given within, and as, forms of repetition. The centrality of repetition provides an approach not just to the presence of function – the reiteration of functions given to be repeated – but also for the interconnection of function, alterity and the differing possibilities for a critical architecture. In order to develop

this position what has to be taken up is the way in which the ineliminability of repetition is linked to the critical. Rather than allowing
for a prescriptive or didactic conception of criticism, the primordality
of repetition means that alterity how to figure within the possibility
of a repetition that takes again for the first time. The paradoxical
nature of this formulation is the consequence of holding to the necessity that the architectural be defined in terms of function, even though
the formal presence of that function and thus the way formal presence effects function are themselves not determined in advance. Built
in to the move to alterity is both the inscription of a level of unpredictability though equally a level where function is retained. In order
to develop both of these possibilities two differing, though in the
related, formulations will be developed.

The first involves showing that unpredictability – chance operating
in relation to constraint – necessitates that certain actual practices
demand an understanding of the architectural in terms of a relationship between the material and the immaterial. This is a position that
is worked out in Chapters 1, 2 and 3. In Chapter 1, it is a position
that is developed in relation to philosophical texts. The argument
involves two moves. The first is the argument that, in spite of its preva-
lence within architectural theory, Plato's conception of 'khora' adds
little to an understanding of architecture once the latter is defined as
the relationship between function and the generation of form. The
second move is to argue that Bataille's conception of 'l'informe' is in
fact indispensable to just such an understanding of the architectural.
Bataille's writings that are ostensibly on architecture are in fact only
ever concerned with the symbolic effect of buildings. The real force
of his work – for architecture – lies in his concern with the generation of form. It is this position that is developed in Chapter 1.

Allowing for the presence of the constraint of function while not
allowing that constraint to determine either form or the particular way
function is understood necessitates the development of a theoretical
argument that allows for the copresence of continuity and discontinuity. Once again the setting in which this movement is to be developed
assumes the primordially of repetition. The overall argument is that
any object that forms a part of the history and practice of architecture achieves this end to the extent that the architectural is retained
as its defining concern. If, however, the critical is defined as a repetition that takes place again for the first time, then while any architectural

object must be such that it forms *a part* of the history of architecture, that object must at the same time be *apart* from the forms of finality demanded by the simple repetition of function. The co-presence of these two forms of relation – marked here by being *a part of* whilst also being *apart from* – is developed in Chapters 2 and 3 though also throughout the book in terms of what has been identified as the logic of the *apart/a part*. The value of this logic is that it allows both for the reiteration of architecture whilst defining the space of the critical – what amounts to alterity in architecture – as internal to the operation of the architectural object.

The work of Eisenman and the projects envisaged by Reiser and Umemoto are different. In writing about them and in deploying a similar structure of argument there is no attempt either to identify or conflate them. The point of contact concerns the way in which design practices are interarticulated with functional concerns. This interconnection allows for a description of the architectural that focuses both on the interiority of architecture as articulated within the interior of specific works. While this project is limited to these two bodies of work it would always be possible to develop this procedure. Fundamental to it, as a procedure, is that it allows for the possibility of judgement within architecture. Rather than making evaluation a purely aesthetic concern, attributing centrality to the complex relationship between repetition and function yields different criteria for evaluation. These criteria are both internal to the history and practice of architecture and just as significantly locate the particular object as the locus of evaluation and judgement.

Judgement concerns the nature of the relationship between the particular and the repetition that it – as an architectural object – is constrained to repeat. Not only is judgement concerned with the nature of the repetition, it is equally the case that the site of critical intervention is itself delimited by repetition. Chapter 1, 2 and 3 develop issues central to the operation of this locus of activity.

1

TIME, FUNCTION AND ALTERITY IN ARCHITECTURE

INTERCONNECTIONS

In a description of the direction taken by some of his recent work, Peter Eisenman identified the central role the interarticulation of experience and form plays within it. While experience emerges as fundamental to his concerns, what is at work is no mere phenomenology. Experience and understanding identify the place of function. His description, with which a start can be made here, is neither didactic nor prescriptive. It outlines a procedure. As a procedure it issues a challenge to architectural theory.

> My recent work has been involved in an attempt to understood how . . . changes in spatial organizations affect our understanding of time and place. This work deals with how this internal time-space relationship affects how we understand buildings and more particularly, how we make plans and facades. Specifically my work addresses the space of difference between the exterior and the interior and the space of difference that is also within the interior. The terms that we use . . . for that space is the inter-stitial.[1] strata (EDGE)

Responding to this challenge means taking up the complex interplay of time and difference within architecture.

Even though difference, in the above citation, is initially limited to the literal difference between the surface or façade, and the interior organization of the building, once these differences are examined then the hold of the literal diminishes. (Indeed, even in the above this move away from the literal is already prefigured in the use of the term 'interstitial' to describe the place between – the place of difference.) Once difference is introduced as an internal possibility within form – sustained by form – these differences become the mark of architectural complexity rather than the simple presence of complex form. Identifying the presence of difference – or architecture's other possibility and thus architectural alterity – is necessarily linked to the development of what Eisenman refers to as the 'time-space relationship'. This relationship needs to be taken up. Pursuing the detail of that 'relationship' becomes the task of architectural theory.

While a concern with space may, at least initially, be unproblematic, time is more demanding. Indeed, if there is a question that complicates architecture then it concerns architecture's relation to time. What is time in architecture? Answering this question hinges on how the relation is thought. The question does not pertain to the relationship between time and architecture. As a question it is both more precise and more exacting. What is of concern is *time 'in' architecture*; answering this question therefore demands paying particular attention to how this 'in' is understood. Any response to the question of time necessitates pursuing that which is opened up by the necessity of responding to the 'in architecture'.

While it may be objected that such an approach is too abstract, precisely because detailing how this 'in' is to be understood would be the same regardless of that which preceded it, such an objection would miss the force of time and its presence in architecture. Time, as will be suggested, is present in architecture from the start. Temporal considerations are already built in. Indeed, it is possible to approach the architectural in terms of built time. What this means is that not only is the object – the built domain – already temporalized by its being located in the complex movement of historical time, the inscription of function and the particular determinations of function engender a series of expectations and possibilities that position the architectural experience in terms of the varying forms of accord that these demands envisage. What is envisaged, and the accords suggested, involve temporal determinations. Moreover, the possibility of there being that critical engagement with repetition which allows for an interruption occasioning the possibility of alterity in architecture has to be thought in terms involving the centrality of time. An interruption within repetition, which here is to be explicated in terms of architecture's positioning of the productive interplay of discontinuity and continuity, is a staging of time. It is not just that time figures within repetition. Rather the complex temporality of objects and their history comprise the different possibilities for repetition.

Repetition opens up function. Moreover, repetition links function and time. While function is always explicable in terms of repetition – functions are given to be repeated – its analysis will always be constrained by the specific and thus the presence of repetition must be accounted for in terms of its detail. This means that the object's relation to function needs to be pursued in terms of a particular relation to the presence of that which is given through repetition. The opening up of repetition and thus the possibility of its displaced retention becomes, as will be argued, the inscription of the future into the present. The future taken on the quality of the yet-to-be and therefore its having this quality rids architecture of the didactic hold of the utopian. This takes place by demanding of the object that it work in terms of the inscribed possibility of the futural – always to be understood as the yet-to-be – into and as part of the building's presence at the present. Opening up temporal complexity allows for the intrusion of alterity into architecture because it both distances the hold of dominance while allowing for the retention of function. The significant addition that needs to be made here, though it is no mere addition, is that the copresence of the yet-to-be and the present neither generates nor has one specific form. There is not, nor could there be an equivalence between any one form and this particular architectural possibility.

What these initial considerations delimit is the presence of a series of relations between time, function and form that resist any straightforward attempt to identify each as single concern. The resistance, in this context, is due to the relations being as much interconnections as they are interdependent definitions. In other words, part of the presence of architecture involves a concern with time, and that time in architecture in working with the complexities of repetition has to be related to the presence of function. Function opens up the question of the nature of its relationship to form. Again precision is vital. It is not a question of whether there is a relation between these elements, but of the nature of already existent relations. The already present – the inscription of the given – is the operation of repetition.

In order to account for the potential complexity at work in these interconnections a particular path has been chosen. In the first place the strictures set by holding to the centrality of the 'in' in the formulation '*time* '*in*' *architecture*' have to be noted. Responding to the set up demanded by these strictures opens up the need to reconsider time and function in the terms they set. The interplay of time and function occasions a more sustained investigation of form. Rather than approaching form as a given in which the homology between form and function is retained as central, two particular elements will be pursued. These elements are central precisely because they occasion the possibility of delimiting the site of the critical within architecture. In the first place, it is the possibility of temporal complexity within architecture. The second is the link between complexity and the theoretical question of the generation of form. Of the many ways form can be taken up for these present concerns it will stem, in the first instance from Plato's treatment of 'khora' in the *Timaeus* and from Derrida's detailed engagement with 'khora', and in the second from Bataille's use of what in his *Dictionaire Critique* he identifies as 'l'informe'.[2] These texts are not chosen by chance not only has each one had an important place in the development of contemporary architectural theory, their own internal concerns – place and the generation of form – are fundamental to any development of that theory.

There are three domains of investigation. The first, which can be more succinctly stated, concerns that which is staged by the formulation '. . . in architecture', and the way that staging opens up questions of time and form. What needs to be identified is the particularity of the architectural. The second domain is concerned with the question of the production of form. The generation of form will be approached, as has been intimated, via a detailed consideration of Plato and Bataille. The terms 'khora' and 'l'informe' have exercised a strong hold on architectural theory. Here they will be taken up within the setting occasioned by the earlier considerations of function and time. Again, what will be central is to identify the extent to which they account for the production of form once form is delimited by having to occur in architecture. This will open up the third domain. Here, for reason that will emerge from the analysis to come, that domain will comprise questions directly concerned with the role of 'l'informe' in architecture.

1   . . . IN ARCHITECTURE

Addressing that which takes place in architecture is already to have taken up the question of time. To be exact, the object of address, at the point of departure, is the copresence of time and place. Architecture is already present. The presence and activity of buildings are impossible to resist. The urban context already determines movement within the city. Architecture and the urban do more than cling to the fabric of existence. They structure activity by providing the places where activities are carried out. As educator or as student, as partner, lover, parent, as doctor or as patient, as manager or as worker, the specific determinations that these positions are given is held in place and thus reinforced by architecture. Architecture works, for example, to hold the opposition between educator and student in place. Structures of pedagogy are already articulated within the architectural setting that they inhabit. A critique of the oppositions identified above may be at its must effective therefore when what is put into question is not the opposition – such a move would lapse into an unending oscillation between idealism and utopianism – but the architecture itself. Real critique, and with it the possibility of a critical architecture, has to be levelled at that which allows for the material reproduction of such oppositions. Criticality emerges therefore in the complex set up in which the differences given within oppositions are retained, though with the possibility that what had been precluded may be sanctioned and that the hierarchies that were to be expected are challenged. The form taken by these possibilities is given within an opening within retention. It is the nature of this opening – an opening to which allusion has been made in the formulation of the already present futurity of the yet-to-be – that has to be taken up.[3]

Nonetheless, starting in this way is to accept the ubiquity of architecture. It is, however, to accept in addition two further aspects of the architectural which are equally as fundamental. The first is that architecture sanctions the repetition of human activity because the inhabited forms occasioning that repetition are already the province of architecture. What this means is that architecture works necessarily within the logic of the gift. Functional determinations are themselves already given. There is an already present conception of the structure of the domestic, or the structure of pedagogy, for example. Structures are already given. Architecture works to allow for the repetition of the already given. While it is necessary to clarify what this claim entails, it needs to be connected to the other area opened up by architecture's ubiquity. What demarcates this second area is the fundamental particularity of the architectural. This point needs to be understood as claiming that architecture is inevitably interarticulated with function or with programmatic considerations. The ineliminability of this interarticulation serves to differentiate architecture from either conceptual art or sculpture.[4]

Ubiquity, repetition and function delimit any attempt to explicate that which takes place 'in architecture'. Detailing the way possible interconnections can occur becomes the task of writing on architecture. Each term stages specific though related questions concerning time. Ubiquity is the all pervasive presence at the present of architecture. This ubiquity generates the question of how this 'present' is to be understood. Repetition is a sustained reiteration of particular determinations. Function, as that which comes to be repeated allows for the question of the temporality of repetition to be made precise, in addition it signals both the locus and the possibility of a specific forms of interruption. This accounts for why there is the question of the temporality of an interruption of repetition. Each of these formulations brings temporal questions into consideration.

While time is always already at work within – and as – architecture the force of these differing questions is they demonstrate that time is not singular. Moving from the simple homology between form and function to the inscription of the yet-to-be as allowing for alterity within repetition is the move away from the possibility of pure singularity. Opening up the impossibility of pure temporal singularity yields the primordality of relation and with it the locus of critique. However operating merely at this level – what would be taken to be simple functionalism – would be to reduce architecture to the differing determinations of function. Form would have been excluded. And yet, it is not as though bringing form into consideration is to add on a hitherto missing element. Form is not an addition to function or function present in addition to form. Form has to be introduced at this precise point. Form can be defined straightforwardly as the relations between volume and surface that enact the building's work as a building. This give rise to a set up where even though form is not to be defined in relation to function such that form is always determined in advance by function and function by form, nor is there the complete absence of relation. Form cannot be separated from function. (The investigative question is therefore the nature and particularity of the inseparability.)

The first part of this formulation of the form/function relation undoes the necessity of that formulation of the relation in which function is taken to dictate form. The second part indicates that while the necessity may have been undone it is not as though form can be considered in its absolute differentiation from function. Forms function. Consequently form has to be understood as the enacted presence of a specific function in a given location.

Considerations of function – that which provide part of this provisional response to an explication of '. . . in architecture' – can be productively linked to the possible intrusion of alterity into architecture. Alterity is the possibility of otherness – alterity – within function. Here, because what is involved occurs in architecture, alterity has to be thought in terms of time and thus not in relation to the intrusion of an absolute other. Alterity is that other temporality possibility splitting the singular, rendering it no more then a mere putative possibility, and in so doing demanding what could be provisionally understood as the housing of a form of interruption; a time which in unsettling the determinations of tradition nonetheless allows for another settlement and therefore another habitation. Time and alterity are interconnected.

Alterity cannot be understood except in relation to the interplay of form and function. Alterity is neither another form nor is it another function or simply another determination of an already given function. Answering the question of alterity in architecture has to be approached in terms of the disruption of homological relation between form and function. Precisely because it is the disruption, rather than the destruction of this relation, approaching the reality of alterity in architecture necessitates having to engage with the question of the generation of form.

Having outlined a number of the elements at work in the formulation 'time in architecture', and having recognized that it is only by holding to this formulation that the possibility and presence of alterity can be addressed, it now becomes possible to take up the question of form. And yet, this is one of the most perplexing questions in architecture. How is the generation of form in architecture to be understood? As has already been indicated rather than answer this question directly, a start can be made with two moments within philosophy that have been concerned to address this precise question. The first is the remarkable section of Plato's *Timaeus* that deals with 'khora', and the second is Bataille's development of what is described as 'l'informe' in his 'Dictionnaire Critique'. Both of these texts have been subject to detailed analyses. In regard to the former the commentary by Derrida has had

a singular impact upon architecture. In regard to the latter the term
– l'informe – often translated as 'formless', has had a pervasive influ-
ence in both architecture and art criticism.[5] While acknowledging the
importance of these two terms within related areas of investigation,
in this context the emphasis is straightforwardly on the architectural.
Therefore what has to be examined are the actual texts themselves
and thus to trace the account offered in both the *Timaeus* and Bataille's
text 'L'informe' concerning the generation of form. The theoretical
question is how these texts would figure in architecture and thus how
the architectural would figure within their own activity as texts.

In procedural terms it is vital to stay with the detail of the texts.
While this may necessitate a certain departure from what would appear
to be directly architectural concerns, detail cannot be avoided. Tracing
the movement of philosophical texts necessitates that attention be paid
to their effectuation as texts. What is central is the way a concern
with form both in regard to its generation and assessment is already
inscribed in the work of these texts. Their own staging of concerns
that could be too quickly cast as no more than their subject matter
opens up possible interconnections between the philosophical and the
architectural. After working through a number of specific arguments,
it then becomes possible to offer tentative conclusions concerning the
way an encounter with philosophical writings on form may allow an
account to be given of how it is possible to maintain that which figures
within the copresence of work and the yet-to-be as a possibility within
architectural practice.

2   KHORA

Plato's dialogue Timaeus has occasioned a sustained commentary, one
which has for the most part been preoccupied with questions of origin
as it has with problems pertaining to space and location.[6] Derrida's
concern with the dialogue is taken to have a significant architectural
component. Derrida's text *Khora* is ostensibly a sustained engagement
with the dialogue; though it is equally an analysis of the place occu-
pied by whatever is staged by such an engagement. The setting of
Derrida's discussion of 'khora' – a term conventionally translated as
place and described within the dialogue as 'ever existing place' (52b)
– necessitates that attention be given to the source namely the *Timaeus*
itself. A beginning has to be made with Plato's text.

The long speech by Timaeus in which the discussion of khora occurs can be described as an attempt to set out and thus to give an account of the origin of the world. The status of this account, its staged presence within the text, is problematic insofar as while it involves an attempted scientific explanation, it is an explanation that cannot be divorced in any straightforward sense from its also being a theological account. Timaeus, to use his words, 'invokes Gods and Goddesses' (27c). However, what will be argued here is that the account he comes to give, rather than taking the form of an unproblematic history of the origin of the earth, a history in which science and the Gods combine, brings with it a complicating factor. Within the work of the myth and despite its commitment to a form of linear history – the movement from one point in time, namely the origin, to another – the myth's work ends up having to inscribe the presence of an insistent complexity into that account. The presence of this complexity not only works to upset its own formulation of a linear history and thus check the immediate value that could be granted to the myth, it also causes a problem in understanding how both space and place come to be established. The philosophical problem is twofold. In the first instance, it is having to account for the nature of the relationship between the place (or form) that comes to be established and that which while fundamental to its constitution cannot itself bear the form (or occupy the place) that it established. The second problem is whether there are the resources within Platonism to account for the demand; a demand arising from the work of the dialogues itself.

The problem of space, is already present in any attempt to define location. It inheres within such attempts, since any attempt is open to the possibility of having to account for the question's own place – the place of the question of place – and thus of the locality that it, as a question, provides for itself. Once it becomes legitimate to ask – what place is it that generate all places? – then what is immediately checked is the possibility that there could be a place that was itself outside this particular locus of questioning. The significance of this problem cannot be ignored. It goes to the heart of any attempt to identify foundations, the temporal connection between foundations and that which succeeds them and the formal connection between what founds and what it founded. (Formal here has a range of meaning including the most straightforward, namely the extent to which what is founded bears the quality or even the mark of that which founds it.) Within the ambit of this formulation there emerges the problem of the foundation of both law and ethos. The logic of khora demands that their foundation be necessarily dissimilar from either law or the ethical.[7] As such law's necessary absence – perhaps pure violence – emerges as the precondition for law. Even though deciding on the viability of this argument is not the issue what cannot be denied is the force of the philosophical problem. As a problem it must be explicated in terms of its own conditions of possibility. The question is the extent to which khora as the necessarily unlike – for Plato a 'third kind' – figures within architecture.

Prior to starting his own speech, what Timaeus is about to say is described by Critias as 'beginning with the origin of the Cosmos and ending with the generation of mankind' (27a). Part of the account to be given requires a twofold presentation of that which is central to any attempt to think through the determinations of space. Again it is vital to be precise. The point in question concerns space and not at this stage that which occurs in architecture.

The first significant element is the presentation by Timaeus of an account of the origin of space and place. The second is far more demanding as it concerns how it is that space and place are to be understood. In other words, what is brought to the fore is the question which addresses the terms within which the presence of space and place are themselves to be understood. Within this particular set up Derrida's initial questioning begins to hold sway. Having identified a number of different conceptual oppositions – the example given by Derrida is the distinction between logos and mythos – that are situated in relation to khora, but are not the expression of khora itself, Derrida then asks the question that deploys the logic of khora:

> how is one to think the necessity of that which, giving place (*donnant lieu*) to this opposition, as to many others, seems sometimes no longer to submit itself to the same law that it situates. What of this place? (*Quoi de ce lieu?*)
>
> (90)

Even if the detail of this passages is left to one side what it announces is the problem of situating, perhaps of placing, that which governs the law of situating and placing. Rather than engaging with the question of how to deduce the existence of such a place the problem would always have to concern what it is that could be said of it. How would it be said? As Derrida remarks: 'What of this place?' Not only is it a place that puts in place the conceptual oppositions through which philosophy takes place, situating itself within the place of its own history while at the same time as providing their ground, it also disrupts the smooth operation of that which has been placed, grounded etc. The occurrence of both becomes the mark of an insistent complexity in the precise sense that what it refers to is a foundationalism that in founding withdraws thereby posing, of necessity, the philosophical problem of how such a ground is itself to be thought. While the acuity of the philosophical problem cannot be denied the question has to be the extent to which what can be readily identified as a problem on the level of the philosophical has an obvious architectural correlate.

Before a return can be made to the architectural – of that which takes place in architecture – it is vital to reiterate the force of the more general philosophical point. The advent of complexity does not arise because of a decision to make the work of space complex. What occurs takes place precisely because that which generates the operative terms within which the philosophical occurs, once present within that which it generates, cannot be – or have been – subject to the regulative principles that it puts into place. (This is the logic of khora.) Within the field of regulation there is an element – identified in the dialogue as a productive element – that falls outside the hold of regulation. Rather than countering regulation with deregulation, the latter emerges as the potentially productive potential not within the former but as always outside it. While this becomes a position that can be sustained within philosophy, what must be maintained as an open question is the nature of its possibility within the architectural. What this question refers to announces as much a distinction between philosophy and architecture as it does a possible point of intersection. If the oppositions defining philosophy emerge from a source that cannot be included within that which it is taken to found, then philosophy – or at least a certain conception of the philosophical – is always indebted to its other. Thinking the ineliminability of that other can become the impetus for another philosophical possibility and thus for the intrusion of alterity within philosophy. This is not Derrida's point, even though it is a conclusion that stems in part from his formulation of what has been described here as the logic of khora. However, within architecture the difficulty in question concerns the incorporation and thus the allocation of space to that which cannot be in place and thus at home. Rather than this other being

the source of architectural alterity, precisely because it obviates any
need to return to the place marked out by what occurs 'in architecture'
it is unclear to what extent khora is an ostensibly architectural rather
than philosophical term. Developing this point further means staying
with the detail of the dialogue.

Perhaps the central Platonic distinction that instructs the discussion
of khora occurs at an early stage in the dialogue. At 28a Timaeus
announces this intricate formulation in the following terms.

> What is that which is existent always and has no becoming? And
> what is that which is becoming always and never is existent?
> Now the one of these is apprehensible by thought with the aid
> of reasoning, since it is ever uniformly existent: whereas the other
> is an object of opinion with the aid of unreasoning sensation,
> since it becomes and perishes and is never really existent.

In many ways this is the standard Platonic distinction between the
externality of the forms (or ideas) on the one hand, and the ephemeral
nature of pure particularity on the other. The eternal forms must, of
necessity, involve a different temporality and ontology to the temporality and ontology proper to mere particularity. The eternal, to utilize
a formulation from the *Cratylus*, must be 'always the same as itself'
(231a), while the particular, on the other hand, is continually subject
to the movement and the process of becoming. There is, moreover, a
mode of perception proper to each element within the distinction. The
eternally existent is apprehended by 'thought' (or reason) while the
subject of becoming is apprehended 'with the aid of an unreasoning
sensation'. Khora is introduced in relation to this distinction. (In any
detailed philosophical engagement with khora the interrelationship
between the term and which occasions its introduction would have to
be examined in detail.) What is, in the end, fundamental to its introduction is that as place its necessity is almost deduced. There has to
be khora. This accounts for why its necessity and thus its place is
established prior to its being named. Whatever it is that khora is
emerges before the use of the name 'khora'. Khora, the word 'khora'
names that movement and process.

In order to understand why this is the case it is essential to
trace the emergence of khora. The reason is that its presence is not
initially self-evident. If there is a distinction, no matter how acceptable

or unacceptable it may seem at this stage, between the eternal and the transient, between reason and opinion, at the basis of which there is the more sustained distinction between being and becoming, why would it be necessary to identify anything other than the opposition itself? This question cannot be avoided. It leads to the necessity of khora since its presence as a question and thus its viability as a question is linked to there having to be a ground of the oppositions that is not itself part of the these founding oppositions. While the inescapability of khora cannon be avoided, that inescapability has to be interpreted in terms of the necessary presence of khora. This necessity has two fundamental elements. The first is that there is a productive dimension to khora. The second is that khora is not positioned within that which it positions. (Again, this twofold movement is the logic of khora.) Asking about the place of khora is therefore to take up the possibility of a different place, a place 'outside' of what it founds. The problematic question is, of course, this founding state of the 'outside'.

Early in the dialogue Timaeus has drawn a distinction between the 'model form' of the cosmos and the 'model's copy'. The important element of the 'model form' is the fact that it is eternal. The model used by the architect to construct the world was necessarily eternal. This is why Plato argues in the same section (29b), that '. . . it [the cosmos] has been constructed after the pattern of that which is apprehensible by reason and thought and is self-identical'.

After having made this claim Timaeus then goes on to announce that the account of the formation of the cosmos in being one remove from the cosmos itself and furnished by humans will always tend to be less than 'self-consistent'. Essential to note is the relationship between the cosmos being 'self-identical' and the impossibility of an account of the cosmos being 'self-consistent'. Even though these terms are importantly different, what they indicate is that there is a self-regulated internality that allows the cosmos to work, and thus a true reflection of that working would have to be given in an account that was for all intents and purposes similar in nature. Timaeus is questioning this possibility. Prior to returning to this moment of doubt it is important to follow a number of Plato's next moves. Having accounted for the world in terms of a copy of the self-identical and thus linked to a version of the eternal, movement has to be introduced. The problem concerns the relationship between the eternal and creation. Plato engages with this problem in a number of places throughout the dialogue. Once of the most compelling occurs in his presentation of the origin of time.

The first element in this account is that the model of the universe is an eternal living creature. Therefore, it is necessary that the universe take on the same form as the model. However, if the living creature that comprises the model is eternal – devoid of any insertion into temporal sequence and thus to that extent atemporal – then it cannot be linked either to what is created, or to what is in the process of being created, or to what is ceasing to be. In other words it cannot be linked to the totality of that which is subject to the movement of creation and destruction. Therefore, there is the need for a movable image of eternity. What provides this is what Timaeus describes as an 'eternal image moving according to number'; in other words it occurs as time. Time therefore becomes an important way of incorporating same and other. Their incorporation involves a necessary harmony which is the appropriate belonging together of that which when taken individually would not accord.

What must be opened up is how this bringing together of same and other does in end, within the heart of the argument, yield khora both in terms of its necessity – hence the reference to its presence having been deduced – and in terms of productivity. The way this argument is staged in the dialogue itself concerns two related moves. The first involves showing that the four elements – fire, water, air, earth, – out of which all things are constructed are themselves sufficiently indeterminate, such that it is impossible to identify them as existing in themselves. They are always in the process of becoming something else. The do not remain identical – i.e. self-identical – in appearance. It is vital to pause here and take up the significance of this possibility. The most important element to note is that of the two categories of existence, namely, *being marked by eternality* (and therefore the subject of thought itself) and *the copy of this model*, (the 'subject to becoming and visible'), when taken together define a set up which while alluded to by the possibility of 'all becoming', also eludes its hold. As such it would need another domain and therefore another space allowing for the existence of 'all becoming'. Part of what makes the possibility problematic is having to define the nature of the alterity in question. (Again, it is essential to remember that while it may be defined philosophically, it remains an open question of whether or not such a

conception of philosophical alterity has an obvious architectural instantiation.) Nonetheless what emerges here is the necessity to establish a
third type of form. It is a 'receptacle' for 'all becoming' (49b). What
has to be underlined is that the need for this 'third kind' is a necessary consequence of the overall argument. Khora is not posited.

The next move is Plato's attempt to reformulate his position. Noting
the lack of enduring fixity in the elements and thus the need to account
for an existence that falls outside the hold defined by the twofold relation to the model – the model itself and the copy – he uses a different
sense of modelling. Here the assumption is that if all figures were
produced of the same substance – the example in the text is gold –
then 'in' asking what a gold triangle is – and here 'is' has to be taken
in its strongest sense – the answer would be that it is gold. It is also
a triangle but its being a triangle is less fixed than its being gold. In
the remodelling it would become something else. What does not change
is the process generating the figures and yet the process, here it is to
be understood as the place of generation, cannot leave it mark on the
figures which come to be produced. This is khora. Plato writes,

> the substance which is to be fitted to receive frequently over its
> whole extent the copies of all things intelligible and eternal should
> itself, of its own nature, be void of all the forms . . . if we described
> her as a kind invisible and unshaped all-receptive, and in some
> most perplexing and most baffling way partaking of the intelli-
> gible, we shall describe her truly.
>
> [51a–b]

That which baffles is described a few lines earlier as 'void of (or
"without", or "outside of" (ektos)) all the forms'. The place of khora
is thus defined. As a philosophical problem the place of khora is thus
delimited. It works in its differentiation from that which it founds. In
being outside the problem of relation the question is how is an outside
to be understood when it is the very outside that generates the opposition between inside and outside. While the resources of Platonism
may reach their limit in an attempt to formulate – or reformulate –
this problem it is not difficult to see that it rapidly becomes the theological problem par excellence. It is the problem of 'absence' that
creates the possibility of another conception of presence; a problem
that perplexes Augustine in the *Confessions* and which determines the

history of negative theology. However, is it an architectural question? A response to this question can only be given after having noted some of the elements of Derrida's own work on khora.

It is impossible to trace the entire movement of Derrida's text. As such it is vital to identify a number of significant moments within it. As the dialogue announces both at the beginning and at the end, to have covered the all – presented all that there is – from its beginning to its end, Derrida locates the inscription of khora – khora as an abyssal moment – within this movement, almost at its very centre. There is however a doubling of the abyss. This doubling approaches what has been identified earlier as complexity. Derrida formulates its presence in terms of an attempt by the text to cover this foundering possibility. It covers by declaring both at the end and at the beginning that the whole story has been told or is to be told. Such a conception of totality – the totality of a completing and thus all inclusive narrative – would, if presented unchecked, hide what Derrida identifies as the 'abyss' or 'chasm'. He formulates this position in the following terms:

> The ontologico-encyclopedic conclusion of the Timaeus seems to cover over the open chasm in the middle of the book. What it would thus cover over ... would not only be the abyss between the sensible and the intelligible, between being and nothingness, between being and the lesser being, not even perhaps between being and the existent, nor yet between logos and muthos, but between all these couples and another which would not even be their other.
>
> (104)

In other words, not only is there an abyss between a series of founding oppositions, there is also the abyss between them – the oppositions – and that which, as he states, 'would not even be their other'. What will this relationship be? What conception of alterity is at work within an otherness that is not simply that of being other, or just as significantly the other of being? These latter questions reveal the presence of a mise-en-abyme in the precise sense that the relationship between khora and the oppositions already figures the relationship between khora and the account of the creation of the world from beginning to end. It figures as a necessary possibility with in it. Derrida's question here concerns the significance of the role this mise-en-abyme plays in the text. He asks,

> Is it insignificant that this mise-en-abyme affects the forms of a discourse on places, notably political places, a politics of place entirely commanded by the consideration of sites (jobs in the society, region, territory, country) as jobs assigned to types or forms of discourse?
>
> (104)

What this question is asking is of fundamental importance. As has been indicated he is alluding to the following passage from the Timaeus (50d). It is essential to remember that the context is the setting of khora '... if the stamped copy is to assume diverse appearances of all sorts, that substance were in it is set and stamped could not possibly be suited to its purpose unless it were itself devoid of all those forms which it is about to receive from any quarter'.

What can be deduced from the passage from Plato though equally from Derrida's own arguments concerning place, is that there is a pervasive sense of the incomplete. However it is a specific sense of the incomplete. In the case of Derrida's identification of a mise-en-abyme within the dialogue which resists the conception of finality that the dialogue itself may have wanted, this is present as a possibility precisely because of the desire for a type of philosophical closure, though equally because of the way in which philosophical texts operate and thus can be read. What is being staged therefore is a specific encounter within philosophy of a certain conception the philosophical; i.e. that conception concerned with the enacted possibility of finality. Philosophical closure understood as a desire and perhaps as impossible delimits certain forms of philosophical practice. Khora in the dialogue orchestrates a different – even though related – problem.

The limits of khora become the limits of the outside and thus of a conception of complexity generated by a relation. The productive potential of khora was thus always outside. What was produced – what had been generated – was therefore always complete. An identification of the incomplete becomes an interpretation of the desire for completion – an interpretation revealing its necessary impossibility. It does not affect the form of the completed. What this means is that allowing for the incomplete in architecture necessitates the inscription of the incomplete as part of the object's formal presence. The only possibility of a productive link between the presentation of khora within the dialogue and the activity of architecture is if the analogy were between the dialogue itself – the philosophical book – and the architectural object. And yet even this analogy will nor work. The mode of presence proper to the work of a philosophical text and its own inscription of the operation has to do with a strictly philosophical conception of completion. All that could be established would in the end amount a type of affinity. The incomplete in architecture invokes a formal presence. Moreover, the incomplete – in architecture – will have become a temporal as well as a formal term precisely because the incomplete has to be explained in relation to what has already been identified as the yet-to-come. Opening up this possibility and thus opening a complexity that defines the object will be approached here in terms of Bataille's 'l'informe'.

3   L'INFORME

Bataille writing on poetry within a 'digression' on poetry, writing in way that, on the level of content, causes a confrontation with authenticity and thus with having to allow for the possibility of there being an authentic poetry, stages an encounter with architecture that works to undo his own famous entry on architecture in the 'Dictionnaire critique'.[8] While poetry may appear to be distanced from the reality of architecture, it remains the case that within Bataille's digression the two touch because his concern with poetry becomes a concern with the presence of form, though more significantly with the generation of form. This is the reason that texts ostensibly on architecture – and here this includes both the text 'Architecture' as well as 'L'obèlisque', 'Le labyrinthe' and 'Musée' – need to be distanced from a concern with the architectural once the architectural is understood as the problem of the generation of form.[9] (They can, of course, also be reintroduced once form has been considered.) The texts on buildings and monuments occurring within Bataille's writings raise different though related problems. What emerges from an analysis of those texts is the question of the extent to which such a site – the monument or building – can be sustained as the locus of counter investments perhaps even of symbolic reworkings. What this means is that the building is viewed as having a symbolic dimension and it is this symbolic dimension that determines the building's meaning. Operating on the level of meaning – the building as sign – is to defer ostensibly architectural questions since what occurs with the centrality of the symbolic is the deferral of any attempt to connect signification and form. A concern with signification in architecture can only emerge once the generation of form has been attributed centrality.

The centrality of the symbolic and thus of the attempt to strip the symbolic of its power governs the 'sacrilege' enacted by Simone as an integral part of her confession taking place within the 'récit' *L'histoire d'oeil*. Masturbating within the confessional is an affront to the site. The complicity of the priest reworks the site. However even though its symbolic determinations may have been checked by the affirmation of a form of auto-eroticism the architecture is left untouched. In other words, masturbation and the inexorable slide towards eroticism do not engage with form and thus with the architectural problem of the interrelationship between form and programme. Within the confines of the récit form is only ever an appearance and thus the bearer of meaning. Indeed, the question of form as the continual place of a repositioning and thus of a reworking or redescription plays an important role within that text. Sir Edmond's own redescription of the elements of the Eucharist holds form in place. Form can be reformed. What is removed from any consideration however is the question of the generation of form:

> the wafers ... are nothing other than the sperm of Christ in the form of (*sous forme de*) a small white cake.
>
> (OC, 1: 63)

What this means in this instance is that architecture, the architecture of the church, as with the wafers, endures without any consideration being given either to the nature of form, or to its production. Hence it could be conjectured that there is no real confrontation with the architectural but only with the symbolic dimension of the building and thus with its meaning. The building as symbol cannot be conflated with the building as the organization of space. A building is both; their relation is important. There is however an important difference. This difference has become obscured in Bataille's formulation. Rather than it staging the interarticulation of programme and form, they have been separated. What this means is that architecture comes to be abandoned as a concern in the texts that take architecture as the ostensible object of analysis.

In the his text *L'expérience intérieure* Bataille, in his digression on poetry, defines poetry as the move from the known to the unknown. The sacrifice of both the referent and the conventions and expectations of usage occur in a relentless drive towards the yet-to-be-defined. This is the space of the literary. Sacrifice and thus poetry are opposed within Bataille's writings to the law, to morality, in sum to what he describes as 'project'. And yet the opposition is not absolute. Whatever it is that marked out by terms such as 'sacrifice', 'ecstasy', 'nudity' etc., it is operative and thus present as workful within the presentation of work. Each of these terms once understood as staging certain process or types of activity resists the possibility of a simple reduction to the literal. Poetry understood as the negative, the power of the unknown, demanding to be maintained as the unknown and thus as the always to be defined, insists on – also within – its own presentation and its being present within words, within the very words that are the place of 'project'. (This state of being 'within' is precluded by definition from the logic of khora. The logic locates production outside even though the narrative of khora and thus its own having been produced may have been incorporated into Plato's own account.) Bataille articulates the position of what can be described as anoriginal complexity with disarming clarity.

> The plan of moral is the plan of the project. The contrary to project is sacrifice. Sacrifice takes on the forms of project, (*tombe dans les formes du project*) but in appearance only.
>
> (OC, V: 158)

These two moments, working with a concern for the literary, reach beyond themselves. They call attention to that which works the possibility of presentation itself; presence as form. In this context this has two direct consequences. The first is the impossibility of pure destruction; the nihilistic gesture that is also found in the promulgation of complete fragmentation (the critique of unity as the positing of a literal *disjecta membra*.) Equally, however, it opens up the possibility of defining alterity in terms of an engagement with appearance. The questions arising with these consequences not only concern what is meant by appearance but whether or not the presence of poetry or sacrifice mediates appearance. In the latter case appearance would no longer be merely appearance. It is the possibility of this mediation and thus for appearance to bear the mark of the power of the negative that is at its most exacting within architecture because of the way in which architecture is present. The analogy between architecture and poetry is not being precluded but rather can only be retained if it is defined in terms of the particular ways both may sustain the productive presence of a negativity resisting negation.

Bataille's recognition of the necessary retention of words, of order, of syntax and sentences, needs to be understood initially as a defiant stand against nihilism. However, for Bataille's own undertaking to be successful, this can be the only sense given to appearance. When he writes of 'the forms of project' there is only one sense in which poetry can have this quality. Again, the word 'form' engenders the same problem. What has to be argued is that neither appearance nor form are either appearance or form if the latter are understood as superficial effects. Rather, they denote the presence of an elementary materiality; words and their sustained unfolding. Indeed, this occurs at that precise point where it becomes possible to identify not the meaning of Bataille's writings but their signification. The latter being the relation that they have to their own material presence. Both as a book and as writing *L'expérience intérieure* works to escape the opposition of appearance and depth by producing from within itself the very openings, fissures, delays and thus experiences that it attempts to present. Its singularity is to be located at that precise point. Its own limits are the limits of its appearance. Neither on the level of form nor appearances does *L'expérience intérieure* appear as a book, or work within the tradition of writing, despite its being a book and the work of writing. Rather than a seamless continuity it becomes – in writing – a complex surface.

What appears therefore cannot be automatically incorporated into a straightforward distinction between surface and depth. This position has significant consequences. The insistence on materiality means that the general claim concerning appearance cannot be generalized. It will already have been marked by an ineliminable specificity. What this entails is that appearance and form become almost local concerns. What becomes fundamental is allowing for the distinction between 'the form of project' and 'project'; and thus between poetry and sacrifice on the one hand, and, mere appearance on the other. Here, this distinction has to be thought in terms of its already involving a productive overlapping.

What this means is that even though the way such a distinction works within the practices of philosophy and architecture always give rise to nuanced decisions and fragile openings, it remains the case that the distinction between 'the form of project' and 'project' is not to be understood as a simple either/or; moreover nor is it the articulation of even a complex relation between inside and outside. Working with their necessarily imbricated presence means, in the first place, insisting on the force of materiality, and secondly allowing for the particular nature of the distinction to be generated by the work's work; in other words by its own self-generating and therefore self-effecting process of realization. It also necessitates recognizing that the work of the negative, what can be identified as a productive negativity, has a certain immateriality. Raising the possibility of an immaterial presence is not intended to introduce an transcendental element into architecture. It is rather that once it is no longer possible to locate the excessive – understood as that which in being in excess of function has a transformative effect on the nature of function – within an element, aspect, or part of the building, then, even though the presence of the excessive has material consequences they will have been produced in connection with what is immaterially present. Excess has broken both its relation to ornament and to harmony by being defined by its relation to that which occurs in architecture. As such excess – to the extent that the word is to be retained – is an opening up of the relation between the material and the immaterial. It will be essential to return to this form of immateriality.

The presence of a process of realization yields economies. In the same way as there is an important distinction between the pure affirmation of the interplay of poetry and project and the simple presence of project, it has to be possible to distinguish between an architecture of project and one in which there is a sustained negotiation with the question of appearance. An architecture of project can be defined as oscillating between the form follows function of conventional modernism and the apparent indifference between form and function characterizing much post-modernist architecture. As such there is the impossibility of pure generality, in the precise sense that it is impossible to conceive of architecture *tout court*. Lacking generality is linked to the question of the essence. What this means is that rather than allocating to the essence a possible determination that is on the one hand unified in nature, while one the other withdrawn from the domain of facticity, the essential becomes the setting of architectures that are always determined by preexisting constraints. What constrains architecture is essential to architecture being what it is. (There inevitable result of this form of argumentation is the move from architecture take as a singular determination to architectures.) The way constraints are instantiated becomes the necessary localization of the architectural; its particularity as already determined by function and programme; i.e. by what occasions the 'in architecture'.

The two working together – the constraint of architecture having to function and the formal presence interarticulated with that function – continue to yield that which is essential to an architectural practice. What this yields is a set up that is marked by an insistent irreducibility; an irreducibility marked by a complex series of interconnections. In the first place, it is the interconnection between dominance and the constraint of function. In the second, it is the link between criticality and its necessary interconnection with a function that is only maintained within the possibility of its being transformed. Given that what is at stake is an ineliminable irreducibility what is demanded is judgement. Judgement does not emerge for ethical reasons. The demand for judgement arises because of an opening necessitating a decision. In broad terms what this amounts to is the claim that what is essential to architecture is that which will always allow for the divide that is at work within Bataille's construal of the distinction between poetry and project.

This set up needs to be opposed to the formulation given to architecture in the famous entry in the *Dictionnaire critique*. Leaving to one side his Vitruvian cojoining of architecture and the body, what endures as central is the specific presentation of form. In this context Bataille raises the question of form in the following way; 'it is in the form of (*c'est sous la forme des*) cathedrals and palaces that the state address itself to and imposes silence on the multitudes' (1: 170). It is in these terms that he situates the storming of the Bastille. What is fundamental to this formulation is the role attributed to the symbolic presence of buildings and thus to their presence as monuments rather than as the ostensibly architectural. Form only occurs in this presentation in terms of providing the symbol; Bataille's formulation is clear, 'it is in the form of . . .'. What this establishes is a distinction between a conception of form that is symbolic and thus works as a monument, and form emerging and thus demanding to be understood in terms of that which generated it. In sum, it is as though form is held within a distinction between building and the monument on one side, and architecture on the other.

Of the Bastille, Bataille writes that: 'the taking of the Bastille is symbolic of this state of things: it is difficult to explain the movement of the crowd, other than by the animosity of the people against the monuments which are its veritable masters' (1: 170).

The taking of the Bastille is linked, necessarily, to the symbolic presence of the Bastille. The Bastille was construed as a monument. The struggles was against the specificity of its monumentality. The link between the monument understood as a building and architecture becomes a particular problem that cannot be addressed by equating each of the elements within this complex formulation.

Once it becomes possible to open up a consideration of form as that which is produced rather than linking architecture to monumentality – a linkage in which all architecture, in the guise of building, runs the real risk of being condemned as essentially oppressive – it then becomes necessary to link that movement to Bataille's own conception of a productive negativity. Form has to be connected to another type of production. The important point here is that criticality, as has been suggested, does not reside in a didactic architecture but in the consequences of the interarticulated copresence of the material and the immaterial. The immaterial brings with it the work of the negative. Holding to the 'im ...', holding to it beyond the hold of the logic of negation, holding its negativity as productive, opens up the possibility of reworking of alterity within architecture. The stimulus comes not from Bataille's work on architecture itself, but from texts taking as central the problem of the generation of form. Fundamental here is the text 'L'informe'.

Initially published in *Documents*, again in the Dictionnaire, this short work, thirteen lines long in Volume 1 of Bataille's *Oeuvre Completes*, touches on the issues central to the architectural.[10] Bataille describes the 'informe' as,

a term working to undo/disturb/rearrange, demanding generally that each thing has its form/the form proper to it' (*'un terme*

*servant à déclasser, exgieant généralement que chaque chose ait
sa forme').*

(OC, 1: 217)

While it will be necessary to continue to return to the text, initially
the key is the process identified by the term *'déclasser'*. The second
moment has to do with the other demand that 'l'informe' brings with
it. It is signalled in the claim that, 'it would be necessary, in effect,
in order that academic men are content, that the universe takes form.'
For Bataille the project of philosophy – perhaps only philosophy as
project – is ineliminably linked to establishing and maintaining form.
The final point, and it could be argued that it is a point that reiterates the movement of declassifying, is that responding to this set up
involves neither destruction nor the positing of the utopian but a
counter affirmation: '. . . affirming that the universe resembles nothing
and is only informe comes back to saying that the universe is something like a spider or spit'. The last point is in the end the most
revealing. It comprises the moment at which, it could be argued that,
Bataille comes to misrepresent the 'informe' by seeking to represent
it. Or rather in representing it – in literalizing it – its structuring force
is betrayed.

Perhaps the greatest temptation with the term 'l'informe' is to
consider it as the simple opposite to 'la forme'. Opposition here would
mean that whatever pertained to one would necessarily not pertain
to the other. While it appears to be only a philosophical concern and
not an architectural one, the central question here is how is the 'in
. . .' of the 'informe' to be understood? Despite the gesture towards
the philosophical this is also the central architectural question. One
possible way of understanding the 'in . . .' is as a negation that allowed
for its own negation. The move to form would occur with the negation of 'l'informe'. However when Bataille suggests that one of the
function's of the 'l'informe' is to bring about a change in register and
thus reposition the exigency linked to form, then part of that process
will be the distancing of the opposition between 'la forme' and 'l'informe' understand as a mutually excluding either/or. What reemerges
at this precise point is the analogy with poetry. Poetry sustains
language, it works with words, meanings, syntax, etc., all of which
are given; more significantly they are given to be repeated. Here the

analogy with the architectural occurs because of the retained presence of the logic of the gift. Within the terms set by this logic there is an interconnection with the exigency that architecture must function. As architecture becomes sculpture, for example, it ceases to be architecture. While the limit condition may define the architectural at its most emphatic, it remains the case the architecture will always have to hold its self apart from other generic possibilities. Again, to the extent that architecture moves towards the condition of conceptual art it ceases to be architecture.

Staying with the analogy with poetry means having to allow for the possibility that there is an analogue within architecture for that state of affairs in which within poetry there is the continual movement between the '*connu*' (known) and '*inconnu*' (un-known). One does not negate the other. More importantly within poetry the insistence of the 'inconnu' – and within the 'in . . .' of the 'inconnu' it is vital to hear the work of a productive negativity – works to hold the form of the already given in place. At this stage a more detail argument becomes necessary on the role of 'l'informe'. The point of connection is between the work and the presence of the 'inconnu' and its rehearsing the productive position of 'l'informe'. Both bring into play a staging of the incomplete and thus allow for a positioning of the architectural in relation to time. In temporal terms what this means is that even though the building is built, despite the fact that it is complete, it remains, at the same time, incomplete. Given that the incomplete works with the complete, since both occur simultaneously, then what this entails is the copresence of a material condition – the complete – that is always working with that which is immaterially present namely the continual condition and conditioning of the incomplete. They are present in their difference generating a complex architecture. Complexity in architecture therefore has to be a consequence of the work of the 'l'informe'. This position can be developed by returning to the text as an entry in a dictionary.

The text – 'Informe' – occurs not just in a dictionary but in a 'Dictionnaire critique'. Bataille is aware, from the start, of the importance of the difference made by the addition of the word 'critique'. While it is not addressed explicitly in these terms, the force of the distinction is articulated in the opening of the entry 'Informe'. There Bataille writes that;

A dictionary begins from the moment when it no longer gives the meaning but the tasks of words. (*Un dictionnaire commencerait à partir du moment où il ne donnerait plus le sens mais les besognes des mots.*)

(OC, 1: 217)

The contrast therefore is between '*le sens*' (meaning, sense, predetermined way, direction) on the one hand and '*la besogne*' (work, task, job, workfulness) on the other. What is being staged here concerns far more than two different senses of dictionary, that limitation has already been rendered problematic by the nature of the distinction already posed between meaning and work. What then does this distinction bring with it? Answering this question is not mere exegesis. It involves working with, by having accepted the primacy of, the text's materiality.

What then of the contrast between meaning and work? In the context of the entry 'Informe' the distinction is developed in the next line of the text in terms of a distinction between the 'informe' understood as an adjective, and 'informe' as workful. Even though the passage has already been noted, it is essential grasp the distinction between the term as an adjective as thus as part of the domain of *sens* and its presence as yielding work.

'a term working to undo/disturb/rearrange, demanding generally that each thing has its form/the form proper to it' ('*un terme servant à déclasser, exgieant généralement que chaque chose ait sa forme*'.)

(OC, 1: 217)

In this context the detail of the term's work is not central. None the less attention should still be paid to the consequence of this process of 'undoing', 'moving' and 'repositioning' (recognizing the difficulty of translating '*déclasser*'). It results in a state of affairs in which the opposition between form and the formless (the latter as no more than that which could be counter posed to form) is no longer appropriate as a way of accounting for form. The presence of form (or its opposite – the so called formless) is not central. The terms are not in strict opposition. What arises as the more demanding problem is accounting for the generation of form.

Before proceeding with the text 'Informe', it is vital to note that an important shift takes place within it. There is a move from what is – i.e. the giveness of a form – to what becomes or to what is generated. This is the consequence of the move from meaning to work. Finitude yields its place to a specific modality of becoming. However, because what has also been displaced is the structure of the either/or, here it would have been present as the opposition form/formless, finitude and becoming are not mutually exclusive. As a consequence two interrelated tasks arise. The first concerns the primordality of relation entailed by the absence of the mutually exclusive. While the second concerns giving an account of the nature of the copresence of finitude and becoming. In sum, pursuing these tasks involves recognizing that what is at work here is that conception of the ontological in which the productive presence of a founding complexity has to be taken as the point of departure. Not complexity understood as Leibniz's 'infinite folds of the soul', but one in which what insists is the origin; the origin understood as the productive copresence of ontological registers which are necessarily irreducible. Production is linked therefore to the anoriginal presence of a differential ontology. Production is the measure of its work. Allowing for the productive interplay of finitude and becoming opens up the need to describe what is being staged within such a set up. The demands made by Bataille's formulations enjoins a task that necessitates a philosophical thinking that begins with the event of plurality.[11]

The work of the 'informe' – the verbal form *'servir à'* ('works to/functions in order to . . .') marking the presence of the ineliminability of work – is already set in place. Its not just that its meaning is its work, thereby eliding the distinction between a concentration on meaning as opposed to work, equally as significant is the fact that this work takes place in relation to the given. It works to reposition the given. In other words, it undoes, by reworking, both the hierarchy and the opposition within which form is assumed to be present. The assumption of form cannot be differentiated from ignorance concerning the nature of form. The 'informe' works to undo, by exposing that which is inherent in the practice of form where that practice is understood as no more than the mere reiteration of form's necessity. It would be a reiteration in which the question of form's production would have been systematically excised. Working with the 'informe' turns attention away from the repetition of form as a given and thus it is, at the same time, turned away from the hypostatization of form. It is in the terms set by this opening that form can emerge as a question. Again, with the question of form, with form present in terms of the question of its production, what is distanced is the opposition between form and formlessness. What emerges therefore is the philosophical problem of how form is to be thought. Any response must begin with the recognition that the enforced abeyance of the opposition form/formless yields a possible move form the oscillation between presence and absence to the centrality of production and becoming. In other words, the question of thinking demand a concomitant shift in how the ontology of the object – and thus how the object – is itself to be thought.

After allocating a specific form of activity to 'l'informe' the dictionary entry then reiterates the distancing of *sens*. The entry continues with the claim that whatever the term 'designates' – what set up the term identifies – its legitimacy is not secured by the work of *sens*. In other words, *sens* and here the oscillation within the word between meaning and direction must be allowed to endure, does not provide the term's force. There is a fragility however in that the possibility that can be attributed to 'l'informe' is easily crushed. Bataille uses an analogy to make the point:

and becomes crushed everywhere *like a* spider or an earth worm.
(*se fait écraser partout comme une araigné ou un ver de terre.*)
(My emphasis)

While the analogy introduces a complication in that it demands an investigation as to its own viability, here that need not be the central issue. What is of fundamental importance is both the distancing of *sens* and the recognized fragility of what ever it is that the 'l'informe' may in fact be. One immediate response to this fragility – thought it is not a response that can be described as coming unproblematically from the text – would be to argue that the fragility occurs because the move leading to the hypostatization of 'l'informe' would involve its inevitable destruction. This would occur because it would involve a shift from work and therefore from 'l'informe' as productive, to a concern with the term as a mere word and thus to defining it simply in regards to its meaning (*sens*) and therefore to the way (*sens*) determined for it. Maintaining the workful nature of 'l'informe' means having to give expression to that which is implicated in its being maintained. In other words not only is there the general question of the relationship it has to form there is the more general question of an ontological description of 'l'informe'.

These two questions are addressed in the next lines of the text. After the claim that there is a desire within the academy for form, this claim is then is linked to a more general one concerning philosophy. Philosophy is construed as having form as its final goal; and here form needs to be understood in terms of both finality and completion. The description of the threat to 'l'informe' that occurs straight after – a threat that would need to be seen as stemming for the academy and thus from philosophy as 'project'- is linked to a description of the ontology of 'l'informe'. It is an ontological set up that both philosophy and the academy would seek to deny. The lines in question are the following:

> It is necessary in order that academic men are content that the universe take form. Philosophy has no other goal: it is a question of giving a frock coat to that which is (à ce qui est), a mathematical frock coat.
>
> (OC, 1: 217)

The 'mathematical frock coat' becomes the imposition of form. It is imposed on 'that which is'. However, it is not as though the absence of form is the alternative. Again, this is why the translation of 'l'informe' by 'formless' simply fails to address the potential the term contains. If, to return to the point already made, 'l'informe' undoes the presumed relation that form has to 'that which is', or the form taken by 'that which is' – in other words it undoes the logic of the gift – then its presence within the inevitability of form must have a transformative effect on what there is. What emerges as a real possibility therefore is that 'l'informe' forms. Allowing for its continuity is to hold to the copresence of form and 'l'informe' and as such to maintain the power of the negative. Whatever 'l'informe' marks out, it is not that which always is negated, of necessity, by the presence of form. (To reiterate the formulation already used in the discussion of poetry; it may be that form is form – the form demanded by philosophy – in appearance only.) That 'l'informe' can be negated by the presence of form is the mark of a persistent fragility; that it need not be is the productive potential of the work of 'l'informe' and as such it marks the possibility of a transformation both of the particularity of form as well as the nature of form itself.

4   L'INFORME IN ARCHITECTURE

What then is the 'l'informe' in architecture? Any attempt to answer this question has to begin with the utility of 'l'informe'. It works. It works to undo a particular given formal determination; not to end up with simple formlessness but with another formal possibility. It works this way by its being maintained. The difficulty here is trying to answer the question concerning the presence of 'l'informe' in architecture in relation to the identification of abstract qualities. Therefore, in order to situate the response to this question some of the recent writings of Peter Eisenman will serve as the point of orientation.[12] There are two reasons why the work of this architect is to be used. The first is the more general methodological clam that consistent with what has been argued thus far there cannot be an adequate abstract answer concerning the presence in architecture of 'l'informe'. Any investigation must always investigate particularity. The second is that beginning with Eisenman allows for an opening in which an important connection can be drawn between alterity and sustaining the presence of 'l'informe'. His architecture is almost invariably concerned with the complex interplay of production and disruption. And in his architectural practice there is the affirmed retention of the yet-to-be, where the retention and with it the inscribed futurity are determined by an engagement with function.

Writing of Bramante's project for St Peters, Eisenman reformulates Bramante's transformations of formal qualities in terms that concentrate on 'modification'.

This transformation of what could be called *poché* from an inert mass between forms, or as something from which void is cut, and to something highly mobile and volatile can be seen as the subversion of the form of both traditional solids and their traditional organization in space. This modification of the material condition can be given a new name – the interstitial.[13]

Here the interstitial is both the condition of the between and the consequence of a particular process. As such it could be described as both process and effect. And yet it is not one and the other – process *and* effect – as though they could be separated. Present here is the inscription of that element – an element whose presence can only be explicated in terms of particularity – whose work is both. This description needs qualification. What are these transformations? There is no suggestion here that all any transformation would involve is a reiteration of manoeuvres similar to the one enacted by Bramante. Such a move would only reintroduce an envisaged homological relation between form and function. Even though a great deal is to be learned from a detailed study of such transformation, the point remains that it is essential that the transformation not be understood as literal. Eisenman's point is both a historical one in terms of how the history of architecture can be read in terms of transformations on the level of formal possibility. More significant, in this instance, are the design consequences that arise from pursuing the interruption and displacement of the conceptual oppositions – the tropes – through which architecture works. Eisenman is after the interstitial as the generative between.

In a description given by Eisenman of his project for the United Nations in Geneva. The aim of the project was to deploy the interstitial – understood as the twofold of process and effect articulated through architectural tropes – 'to destabilize the traditional social organization of any program'. The initial object was '. . . to destabilize the ideas that buildings are containers of meaning, structure, and functions, dependent on their visual recognition as such'.[14]
Initially, the key term in this passage is 'dependent'. There is no attempt to undo the presence of either structure or function. What is central is the access that is given to structure or function. What is being undone is what has already been described as the homological relation between form and function. The interstitial as deployed in the project works – and the work would need a formal and detailed description – to break that homology. The break is not the move from form to the formless. On the contrary it is to reintroduce into the presence of form an indeterminate quality which alters the perception and practice of the building while at the same time allowing for programmatic possibilities that had not been determined in advance.[15]
What is of concern is how in this context is the interstitial established.

Fundamental to the position being developed is his argument that the object is structured through a transformation of the conventional oppositions given to architecture. The transformations occur within and thus come to be 'housed'. Transformations are both internal and yet constitutive of the internality itself.

Even though it involves reiterating a position already stated, Eisenman's own description of the interstitial is of great significance. It is not just that within it there is an important gesture to arguments central to Bataille's conception of 'l'informe', it is also the case that this interior spacing involves the active presence of time. Allowing for that activity means that spacing takes on a workful quality. As such what insists is the ineliminable question concerning the nature of that work.

> My recent work has been involved in an attempt to understood how . . . changes in spatial organizations affect our understanding of time and place. This work deals with how this internal time-space relationship affects how we understand buildings and more particularly, how we make plans and facades. Specifically my work addresses the space of difference between the exterior and the interior and the space of difference that is also within the interior. The terms that we use . . . for that space is the interstitial.[16]

Before turning to his description of work of the interstitial in the Aronoff Centre it is essential to be clear about the issues at hand.

As has already emerged both from the above and from the description of the United Nations project, the interstitial as constitutive of internality and of displacing structures of recognition allows an object to take on different temporal possibilities. Explicating those possibilities demands a link between what has been identified as the yet-to-be and the 'l'informe'. As has been intimated, central to the operation of 'l'informe' is its utility. It works to undo. What is undone is the homological relation between form and function. In other words, what it works to undo is an envisaged one-to-one relationship between a given function and the form that it takes. The homology of the pregiven is destabilized by its operation. However, this is no simple undertaking; indeed, it is one that would define the limit condition of architectural practice. The relationship between form and function once rescued from abstraction can be understood as the repetition of certain

fundamental structures within architectural practice and thus in terms
of architecture's expectations and the expectations held for architecture. The site of intervention therefore is a structure, or concatenation
of structures, of expectation. This becomes the site and the possibility
for criticality. Eisenman's description of the United Nations project is
precise. What would have become impossible within its actual realization was an identification of place and thus an identification of
programme as given by immediate awareness of position within the
building.

What is meant by the formulation, 'the space of difference'? From
the above citations the differences in question pertain to the relation
between exterior and interior as well as differences within the interior. The nature of difference is the question. It is unremarkable to
note that there is a difference between exterior and interior. They are
different by definition. What more is being adduced in Eisenman's
formulation? Answering that question necessitates recourse to a specific
project.

The Aronoff Centre at the University of Cincinnati involves an addition to a preexisting building.[17] It is also the addition of a new building
insofar as elements of the new building are distinct from the old.
None the less, there are points where what is central to the building's
operation is the way it negotiates the addition. Eisenman describes the
negotiation as a blurring. He describes the addition in the following
terms;

> Our addition created an interstitial space between the existing
> building and the new building. So as to blur the boundary between
> the two, a contrasting curved form was initially placed next to
> the existing volumes in order to activate the interstitial space
> between the new and the old, capable of pressing, like a balloon
> into both. The expression of that pressure would be manifest on
> the exterior surface and the new interior surfaces of the old.

Generated by the addition was a third term. There emerged a condition that could be reduced neither to the presence of the old nor to
that of the new. It arose from within their relation. The spacing which
both divides and relates the exterior and interior is such that in this
instance it generated another possibility; a possibility with material
presence. This occurred because of the nature of the relation between

an exterior space that came to be incorporated and an interior space that was properly that of the addition. As such, this gave rise to a set up in which the viability of terms such as exterior and interior lose their purchase if taken to define in an absolute sense the occupation and programmatic effect of the building. (In part what is taking place is that these terms can no longer be defined literally. The place for that possibility is not architecturally present.) And yet, the displacing of the opposition exterior/interior does not mean the vanishing of the object. On the contrary, the insistence of its presence demands a reconfiguration and thus theoretical reexpression of its constitutive elements. That reconfiguration occurs here due to the way the elements are brought together.

In Eisenman's formulation a similar state of affairs occurs in regard to the opposition between new and old. It is essential to note the way a certain utility is being attributed to 'interstitial organization'. This gives rise to two demands; that an account be given of both this utility and its being the work of spacing.

On the inside the same interstitial organization is proposed in order to blur the distinction between new and old where new pushes into old and old into new. The different energies that cut through from the interstitial space are also marked on vertical interior surface from pieces that have been inserted between the old and the new.

What is being staged here is straightforward. The interstitial as the space of difference operates by undoing the 'tropes', usually present in terms of binary oppositions, through which the conventions and the expectations held for architecture operate. The space of difference is no longer that of literal differences but the one in which the hold of the literal has diminished such that exterior/interior and old/new can be brought back.

What this means is that the interstitial understood as the space of difference has an effect. It is not a simple 'between'. What it disrupts can be explained in terms of expectations. None the less, the essential point is that in disrupting the homology of form and function the quality that is produced – the third term that is there as an unpredictable consequence – cannot be determined in advance. It is not empty space awaiting programmatic injection. Rather the complex activity of spacing produced that which is yet-to-be determined. In the case of the Aronoff Centre it is not there as an addition, but by the way the addition caused a destabilization of the determinations of exterior and interior. There is a further element that has to be added. Once it can be assumed that what is at work is a relationship between a certain sense of determination and thus the allocation of programmatic possibility within a building whose function is already explicitly stated, then the yet-to-be while defined in relation to programme introduces two complicating elements. The first is that it brings a certain sense of plurality into play. The building take on the quality of that which is both determined and the yet-to-be. In fact this has to be the case. Once the homological relation between form and function is broken, then in lieu of an architecture of prescription what occurs is the inscribed presence of a future whose field of operation is the present.

The already determined and the yet-to-be cannot be reduced to each other. It is terms of the ineliminable plurality – an anoriginal irreducibility – that the building can take on the quality of a plural event. The second complicating element is that the interplay between determination and the yet-to-be staged by the building as its work, means that the work is then defined by the interplay of finitude and becoming. Finitude is the attribution of content and programmatic specificity. Becoming is at work both in the continuity of the realization of the finite, though more importantly in the maintained presence of the yet-to-be where the latter is understood as the continual opening within the building's work.

Eisenman's formulation of the interstitial brings two different elements into play. The first is the disruptive quality. In disrupting what is retained are the functional and programmatic elements. They are, however, retained in their transformation. This brings the second element into play. The interstitial causes terms such as 'interior', 'exterior', 'surface', 'new', 'old', 'void' etc., to break the hold of the literal and thus operate in different ways. Again, these differences cannot be determined in advance. In addition these two senses of disruption preclude the possibility of reading the building from its surface. It becomes a series of layers opening out, holding, yielding and awaiting. No longer simply between, the interstitial is now concerned with forming the between. Indeed it is within this formulation that it becomes possible to trace Bataille's concern with the generation of form.

Once architectural concerns are delimited by the generation of form and the maintained presence of the critical, then there has to be both production and disruption. In Bataille the latter is there is the practice and work of poetry, Equally, it would be the other possibility for the work of 'l'informe'. For Eisenman, criticality in eschewing the prescriptive has to allow for the integration of alterity into the building's work. Alterity and the critical are always marked by a present futurity. This becomes part of the complex process of the interstitial.

In conclusion; what has be identified here is the twofold movement of production and disruption. It is at work in Bataille's conception of 'l'informe' and in Eisenman's conception of the 'interstitial'. Both terms attest to the impossibility of separating form and function. Moreover, the interplay of form and function locates the site of production and disruption. In more general terms what this means is that within architecture – to the extent that architecture is sustained – neither destruction nor nihilism are real possibilities. Sustaining architecture means that it is impossible to be against architecture. Alterity, therefore, is defined by the terms set by the form/function relation. Accepting that setting and in so doing to eschew both destruction and the utopian is to accept the site of architectural alterity as given by that relation.

Complicating this conception of alterity is its having been delimited by a form of acceptance. Alterity is disruption and thus it involves a distancing and a positioning that is necessarily apart from the homological relation between form and function. And yet, at the same time, accepting means the retained presence of function such that alterity is also delimited by the presence of that which forms a part of the functional determination in question. There is therefore a primordality of relation. A relation both thought and positioned within the operation of repetition. Alterity therefore is only possible to the extent that there is the retention and the transformation of a particular function. Both are necessary since both determine the locus of alterity. Since both are essential what yields the possibility of alterity in architecture is the twofold possibility of that which distances – the *apart from* – occurring at the same time as that which sustains the constraints given by remaining in architecture, namely that which forms *a part of*. This set up – the logic of the apart/a part – has two consequences. The first is that alterity is always defined by relation and repetition. The second is that arguing for the presence or absence of alterity can only be undertaken on the level of the particular. Of any plan or building the

2

RESISTING AMBIVALENCE

FORM AND FUNCTION IN EISENMAN'S ARCHITECTURE

There is a particular project within architecture that can be linked to the name Eisenman. What marks this project out is a complex doubling of repetition. Understanding the nature of this doubling opens up the different projects within which it is incorporated. Repetition is not being adduced; architecture works within the inescapability of repetition. From the moment that drawing begins, from the inception of a computer generated experimentation aimed at the generation of form, what is being staged is a reiteration of the architectural. Each new activity, insofar as it sustains architecture, stages its own relation to the history of architecture. Even though this position may remain unnoticed by the architect, or even if the architect seeks to forget the determining presence of that relation, neither the drawing, nor the design, let alone the resultant building (if there is one) forget. The work of memory already marks the process. What becomes essential is the extent to which specific architectural works affirm the productive presence of memory. Eisenman's work is for the most part defined by the presence of this form of affirmation.[1]

At its most minimal, however, the implicit work of memory is the work of repetition. Repetition inscribes. What this means is that it is only in terms of repetition that an account can be given for how and in what way any new project is architecture's work. The doubling of repetition occurs because not only does repetition announce the possibility of a continual reiteration of the given, there also has to be an allowance for a form of repetition in which architecture can sustain a specific critical dimension. This latter possibility – this other repetition – occasions both the identification of Eisenman's work, and with that location, that which defines the locus of intervention and therefore what delimits the place of the critical. The critical demands a point of intervention. The contention here is that this dimension is only brought about within his work by a strong relationship between form and function. Indeed, as is argued, this relationship and the accompanying transformation of the particular function, that delimits the reach of Eisenman's practice.[2]

If there is a contrast with this position, it does not just emerge in the reiteration of architecture's conventional practice, either in the form follows function proper to versions of modernism, or the ornamentalization of ornament and thus the apparent indifference between form and function marking much post-modern architecture. There is another contrasting position. It is both more nuanced and more demanding. Standing as an alternative to Eisenman's activity is a position which while distancing the traditional interconnection of form and function achieves this end by bringing with it an ambivalent relation to the critical. In sum, what this other position envisages is a much looser relationship between programme and form. In this instance the consequence of this looser connection is twofold. In the first place, even though the incorporation of a space that is yet to be programmed may provide the possibility for an architectural practice able to enact a functional criticality, the critical would only ever be an after effect. And yet, in the second place, the neutrality – real or not – of such a set up could also mean that the delay in installing programmatic concerns would merely result in the subsequent reinscription of those programme's most traditional determinations. It is precisely this latter possibility – the threat of its realization – that drives the interconnection between function and form in Eisenman's work. Refusing programmatic considerations has a direct consequence. The refusal entails identifying the domain of innovation as the production of form; form as independent of functional concerns. What this set up implies therefore is that rather than a directly conservative relation – a repetition of the Same – or the projection of an interrupted repetition, what would amount to the copresence of continuity and discontinuity, there would be an insistent ambivalence. It would be in these terms that Eisenman's work would need to be understood as an architecture resisting ambivalence. Resistance, rather than overcoming ambivalence would establish in its place a form of deferral. The refused enactment of the programmatic is not the same as the deferral of the complete realization of function. The latter beings with it a different temporality, one hinging on the retained centrality of the incomplete. In this sense deferral involves the copresence of the realization of function which, in not being realized at one and the same time, inscribes futurity into the work of the building.

Strategies resisting ambivalence but which enact in their place complex forms of deferral provide the setting for this treatment of Eisenman's work. A fundamental part of this project involves developing some of these differing possibilities; what unites them is repetition. And yet, because repetition does not admit of an essence, what has to be traced are the different, and in the end incompatible, modalities of repetition and the way in which they are already interarticulated with ambivalence and deferral; the former in contrast to the latter. There is no intention here to make a straightforward claim about authenticity. Ambivalence in architecture remains architecture. What counts, of course, is the nature of the architecture in question.

In this instance the importance of the repetition is that it generates both the site and the possibility of, critical architecture. Criticality is linked to the nature of the repetition. Given that any new work is already a repetition, the question that must be asked would concern the nature of that repetition. As has already been indicated there are at least two divergent possibilities for repetition. In addition to a repetition of the Same – that form of repetition in which tradition's gift, that which is given to be handed on, comes to be handed on – there is another significant type of repetition. The latter possibility is a repetition in which something takes place again for the first time. This is the doubling of repetition. Eisenman has, in his correspondence with Derrida, already identified these two particular modalities of repetition. Eisenman, both as a theorist and as a practitioner is already aware of the complex determinations of repetition. What is of real importance in the following passage is the reliance upon the specificity of the architectural. Its internality is the site from where the possibility of change and innovation emerges. (As will be made clear to insist upon internality is not to insist upon a formulation indifferent to function. Internality will always have the possibility of an inscribed opening.)

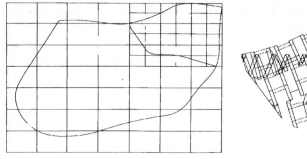

concept diagram, superposition of net

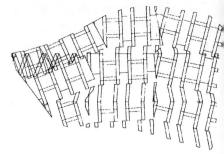

concept diagram, typological fabric

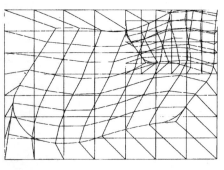

concept diagram, transformation of net

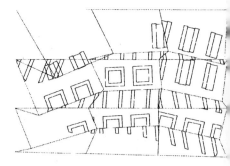

concept diagram, building typology

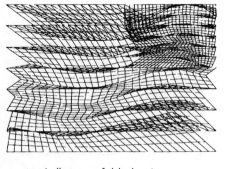

concept diagram, folded net

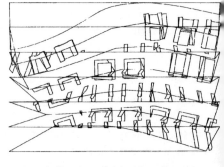

concept diagram, folded typology

Figure 2.1   Rebstock Park master plan

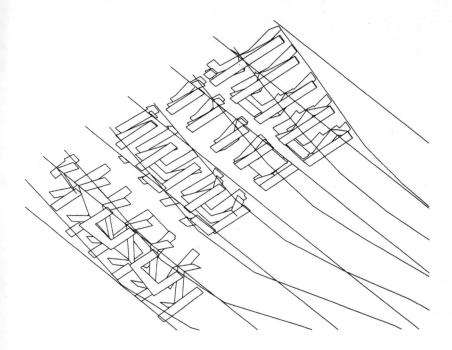

concept diagram, building fabric

Figure 2.2 Rebstock Park master plan

The need to overcome presence, the need to supplement an architecture that will always be and look like architecture, the need
to break apart the strong bond between form and function, is
what my architecture addresses. In its displacement of the traditional role of function it does not deny that architecture must
function, but rather suggests that architecture may also function
without necessarily symbolizing that function, that the presentness of architecture is irreducible to the presence of its function
or its signs.[3]

Via an analysis of the claims made in this passage it becomes possible
to identify both the different forms taken by repetition and the different
openings they occasion within architectural practice. (It is in terms of
repetition that an initial discussion of some recent projects can take
place.) The tight relationship noted above between function and form

is signalled in the passage in terms of the formulation that 'architecture must function'.

The initial claim of overcoming presence is linked to what Eisenman has described in a number of different texts as 'presentness'. (A similar idea continues to work within a great many of his projects and his writings. However, it continues to be given different names.) The force of this term is, in this instance, twofold. In the first place it is used to free architecture from having to work within the constraints established by the conceptual opposition between presence and absence. While in the second, it introduces an ordering process that is generative of form but which cannot be reduced to the simple material presence of a given aspect of architectural work. While it involves straying from Eisenman's proper concerns it will be argued at a later stage that this second element introduces into the material presence of architecture what could be best described as an immaterial force. The immaterial has to be construed in terms of a productive negativity. In the 'im-' of the 'im-material' the work of the negative is being marked out.[4]

Opening what in his letter to Derrida he refers to as the 'strong bond' between form and function allows for 'presentness'. Prior to pursuing the details of this term, it is vital to stay with the passage in question. The starting point needs to be the apparent contradiction arising from the claim already made that Eisenman's work is sustained by a strong relationship between form and function and the position advanced in the letter that his work intends to break the 'strong bond' between form and function. Care is needed here since it is only by opening up the strong bond that the deferral of function can occur. The important point is that with this opening it becomes possible to defer finality by allowing programmatic implications only ever to unfold in the building's own continuity. This deferral, almost the inscription of a workful infinite, takes place within the finite. Finitude means however the retention of a function that in being retained is able then to be reworked. The location of the infinite within the finite not only underscores the necessity of holding to the continual work of an internally located productive negativity, it also opens up the complex presence of time. As will emerge retention, deferral and transformation are all interconnected. Despite certain similarities deferral cannot be automatically identified with the to-be-programmed. On the contrary, it holds to the centrality of function but breaks the link between modalities of function and temporal

concept diagram, folded
wire frame

Figure 2.3 Rebstock Park master plan

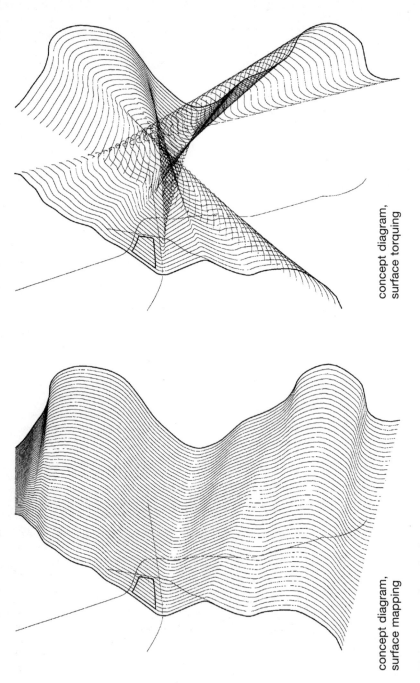

concept diagram,
surface torquing

concept diagram,
surface mapping

Figure 2.4   Klingelhöfer-Dreieck

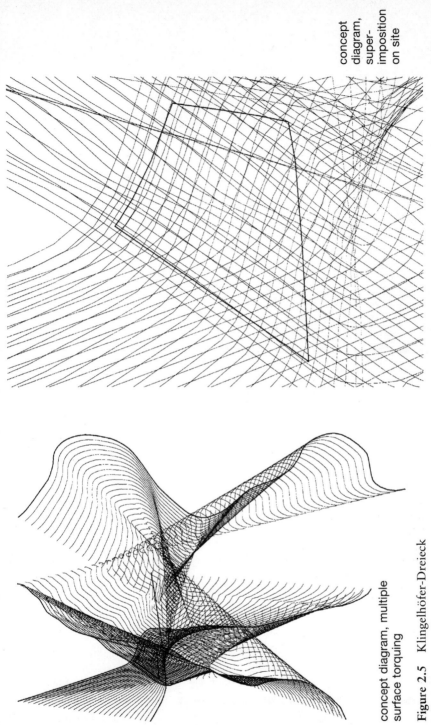

concept diagram, multiple
surface torquing

Figure 2.5   Klingelhöfer-Dreieck

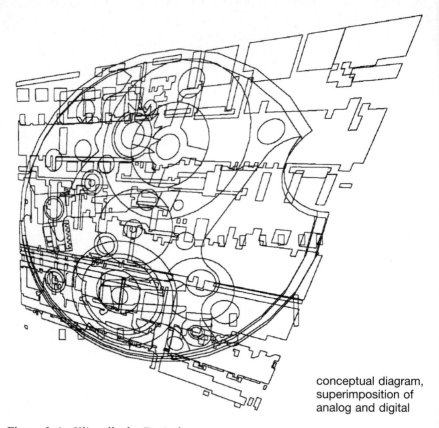

conceptual diagram,
superimposition of
analog and digital

Figure 2.6 Klingelhöfer-Dreieck

presence. The present can no longer be understood as a self-completing finality. The present comes to be structured by the insistent presence of the incomplete which is itself only ever immaterially present and yet materially produced.

What Eisenman means by the 'strong bond' is best understood as the moment where the reiteration of conventional usage is reflected in the form that such usage occasions. Repetition in this instance is determined by the operation of the Same. In other words, it is a claim that function can only have one form because function has a singular nature. What is given to be repeated comes to be repeated. In regards to the museum what this would entail is, for example, a retention of the

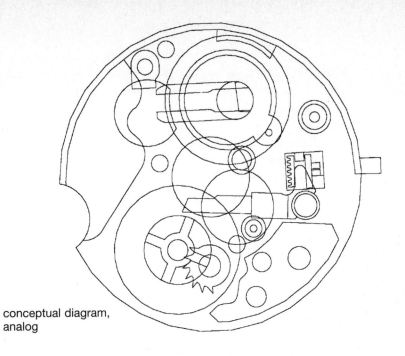

conceptual diagram,
analog

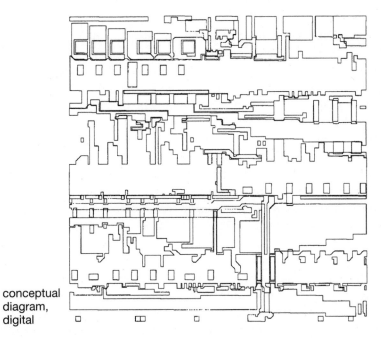

conceptual
diagram,
digital

Figure 2.7   Klingelhöfer-Dreieck

dominance of chronology as providing the museum's internal orga-
nizing principle; or the reiteration of the conventional picture space
thereby determining in advance what can be shown, the space it would
have to occupy and thus what would count as an art object. These
determinations in advance are the ways in which the work of tradition has to be understood. Prior to any comment on this set up, it is
essential to note that fundamental to it is the operation of repetition.
Consequently, when Eisenman writes of breaking the 'strong bond'
marking the interconnection of function and form, this needs to be
interpreted as an intervention within a particular modality of repetition. The intervention in being neither destructive nor utopian aims
to institute another possibility one where the alterity in question – the
otherness of this other possibility – is given by its being a different
conception of repetition. This other conception is announced in the
claim that, 'in its displacement of the traditional role of function, it
does not deny that architecture must function, but rather suggests
that architecture may also function without necessarily symbolizing
that function . . .'. (The 'it' in question is, of course, Eisenman's own
architecture.)

Again, it is important to recognize that in the place of either destruction or the utopian there is 'displacement'. Displacement can be
understood as involving the copresence of continuity and discontinuity.
They must be copresent at the same time. The simultaneity of continuity and discontinuity is fundamental both to the way displacement
operates and to the way it sets in play another form of repetition. It
is in terms of this repetition that displacement allows for the unpredictable. However, the unpredictable does not exist in itself. It is always
strictly delimited by the strong relationship between function and form.
Whatever it is that is unpredictable relates to the nature of the function in question (e.g. museum, domestic house) such that form has to
be linked, within and as the building's work, to sustaining this unpredictable possibility. Displacement figures neither on the surface nor is
at work in the depths. Displacement is driven through the site. Working
from the outside to the inside it displaces surface and depth; in addition, it displaces the opposition between inside and outside. The
complex interplay between displacement and the unpredictable needs
to be pursued.

Displacement is a shift. And yet it is also a type of repositioning.
It names a movement in which continuity is refigured. There cannot

be other than continuity, such is the dictate of repetition. However, it does not follow from the inevitability of continuity that the generic possibility (e.g. museum, domestic house, architecture school) cannot engage with both the ideology and the form that the genre gives to be repeated. Engagement, here would be an intervention into a more generalized site of repetition. Consequently, when Eisenman writes of an opening within repetition – an opening that occurs precisely because of the retention of function and the copresent inscription of another form – time is central. The simultaneously copresence of continuity and discontinuity designates a complex precisely because it generates the presence of a productive irreducibility.

How is the 'irreducibility' to be understood? The first element to note is that the irreducible quality is copresent with that to which it cannot be reduced. That state in which the irreducible is given by its own constitutive elements having to be copresent in their difference, signals the presence of an opening; an insistent though fragile opening. There are two questions here. The first concerns how this opening is to be understood. While the second concerns the extension of this irre- ducibility. Fundamental to any answer that can be given to this second question is the transformation that is introduced by the presence of irreducibility. In other words, the retention of function should not be understood as the simple retention of the specificity of the particular function. Rather functionality is both held and transformed in the same movement, with the resultant possibility that the work in ques- tion becomes the affirmation of a plural event. Plurality, here, refers to the presence of this founding irreducibility. The copresence of the material and the immaterial, for example, brings with it the necessity of having to describe a set up that is from the start complex. Complexity, rather than being semantic in nature – a form of semantic overdetermination – is ontological as it refers to the mode of being proper to this version of the architectural. Ontological complexity rather than being adduced must be understood as always already insisting.

Initially the claim of irreducibility concerns signification. Whatever it is that accounts for the 'presentness' of architecture, Eisenman argues, it is not the same as the meaning – literal or symbolic – of the building. Presentness, that which is irreducible to what is present is 'excessive'. It is worthwhile pausing here to ask two specific and related ques- tions. What is the excessive in architecture? Where is the excessive in architecture? There may be many ways of answering such questions. Excess may refer to colour, and thus it could be located in a contrast of colours. Or excess could involve the use of certain building materials. Equally the sign of excess may have to do with size. This may occur either explicitly or in the juxtaposition of different sizes within the same site. Furthermore, the excessive could be linked to the aberrant, the idiosyncratic or the eccentric. As such the excessive would have to do with quality. Moreover it would be a quality that could be identified either with elements of the building or perhaps with the way the totality conveyed a certain mood.

Further answers of this form can be given; they are all interconnected. What holds them together is that the excessive comes to be located in an element of the building's construction; it may also be present in an aspect of its existence. It may however be the object itself. This eventuality is more likely to be the case if excess and size were linked directly to the object. In each instance the excessive would have to do with literal presence. The excessive – excess in architecture – would be present in either part or whole and therefore could be identified and described as such. It is interesting to note that operating on the level of the hermeneutic – the concern with the building's meaning – there would always be the need to identify the presence of the excessive. In nearly every case the excessive could be delimited. It would refer to particulars uses of, for example, ornamentation or size. The key element would be the literal presence of the excessive. As will become clear Eisenman's use of the excessive counters the identification of the excessive with the literal.

At this point it is necessary to differentiate Eisenman's position from the ones expressed above. All these identifications and locations of the excessive are precisely *not* what is intended by Eisenman's use of the term. How then is it possible to incorporate the presence of the excessive and yet to assert at the same time that it is not present as such? What would it mean to claim that it is not materially at hand? Answering such questions will open up further the complexity within the doubling of repetition.

Here the concerns of the irreducible and the excessive interconnect. It is not difficult to envisage an interpretation of the excessive that links it to a process of ornamentation. What is important is the reason why such a positioning would be incorrect. Ornamentation has to do with actual presence. Presentness or the excessive, in the sense used by Eisenman, does not have an automatic link to actual presence. Rather the operation of the building, its specific internal economy, allows for the identification of function but due to the building's self-effectuation – its own continual realization as the building's work – the presence of that function can no longer be automatically assimilated to constitutive elements of the building's formal presence. What is repeated is the nature of the specific functional and programmatic concerns. The Wexner Centre in Columbus Ohio, for example, functions as a museum. Its presence cannot be divorced from the display of art work. And yet, its being present, the way it works to realize its own programmatic ends, transforms the nature of the museum. The transformation does not occur because of an addition to the museum. It is there as a potential integrated into the detail and the structure of the museum itself. Its integration does not mean that what has been integrated has the status of an ornamental extra nor, as has already been suggested, a carefully staged addition. On the contrary, the transformative capacity is the excessive dimension within the building. It is there within the building's own relation to function. Excess is inherently linked to function and thus to its realization as the building's work. A detailed analysis of the Wexner would be necessary to show the detail of these claims. All that is possible here is to take up in more general terms the work of this modality of presence.[5]

The inevitable reinscription of a use to be transformed means that the generic possibility that yields a particular end is held in place. This is a form of repetition one which locates the building as a part of the generic possibility that it reiterates. Transformation, and in this instance it needs to be added immediately that what occurs is transformation rather than destruction, means that another form of repetition is at work. Now, however, not simply does the building form a part of a specific genre, transformation means that it can only form a part to the extent that it is, at the same time apart from a simple repetition of the genre in question. It must be both. What determines the force of this claim is that the movement of being of '*a part of* . . .' occurs at the same time as that in which the building is '*apart from* . . .'. The doubling of movement brings with it its own logic; a logic repeating the copresence of continuity and discontinuity. It is in terms of the twofold movement marking what the work of *the logic of the apart/a part* that it is possible to stage more concretely important aspects of irreducibility. There are two reasons why this is the case. The first is

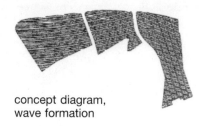

concept diagram,
wave formation

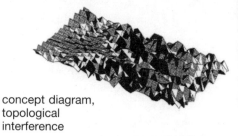

concept diagram,
topological
interference

concept diagram,
isometric of interference

concept diagram,
interference field

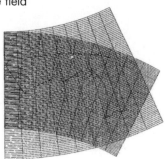

concept diagram,
overlap of wave and
interference

concept diagram,
superimposition of
radar

concept diagram,
context-origin of
interference

Figure 2.8 Nordliches Derendorf master plan

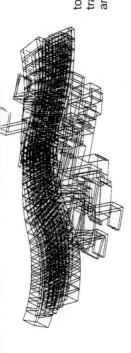

torquing solid and
trace, stepping solid
and trace

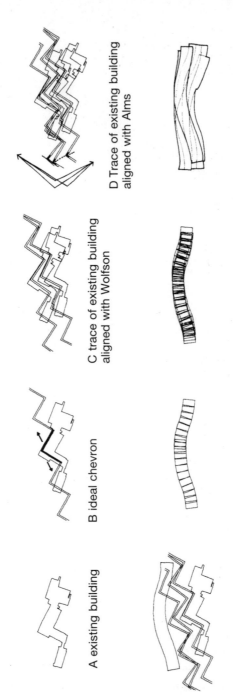

A existing building

B ideal chevron

C trace of existing building
aligned with Wolfson

D Trace of existing building
aligned with Alms

Figure 2.9 Aronoff Center for Design and Art

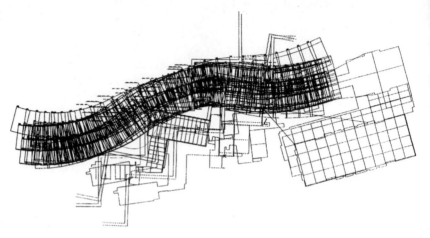

concept diagram, composite curves and chevrons

Figure 2.10   Aronoff Center for Design and Art

that the opening staged by the apart/a part is itself the mark of an enduring irreducibility. The second is that as the logic works in terms of a distinction between the material and the immaterial, what is already being acted out is the very irreducibility that the logic names. This latter point is both difficult and demanding. In sum, however, what the work of the apart/a part marks is the impossibility of escaping the hold of repetition – every work is already a part – and yet the possibility of displacement, transformation – being apart – depends upon an intervention within repetition. Repetition is the already present relationship between form and function. The work of tradition is to hold and reinforce the 'a part' whilst refusing the possibility of the 'apart'. What this means is that the former – the a part – becomes the repetition of the Same while the inscription of the latter – the apart – accounts for the transformative repetition. The important point is, of course, that the possibility of a transformative repetition depends upon the presence of the 'a part'. Hence, what can be identified as the doubling of function depends upon resisting a formal ambivalence.

The presence of the excessive – and this is equally true in regards to the mode of being proper to what Eisenman calls 'presentness' or the 'auratic' – endures with what is present but cannot be reduced to the immediacy of that presence. The immateriality of the excessive is not to be understood as a transcendent quality within the building.

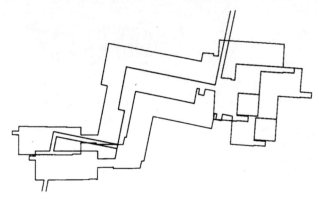

shifted chevron trace

tilted chevron trace

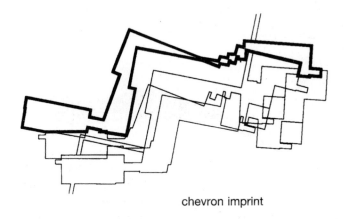

chevron imprint

Figure 2.11   Aronoff Center for Design and Art

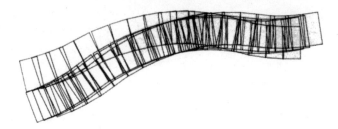

tilted curve trace

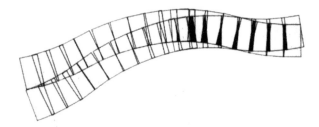

tilted curve trace 400

tilted curve trace 500

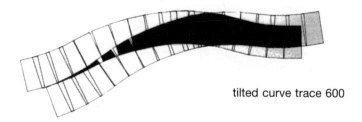

tilted curve trace 600

Figure 2.12   Aronoff Center for Design and Art

Here, the presence of an immaterial productive negativity has to be located within the relationship between function and form; it becomes the particular operation of function. Prior to noting its strategic operations within Eisenman's recent work – The Aronoff Centre for Design and Art at the University of Cincinnati – its presence within a number of recent urban projects needs to be noted.

Initially it would seem to be the case that with the urban projects there would need an initial attempt to establish the nature of the difference between the urban and the single building. While there are obvious and important differences there is a significant point of connection. In the case of single buildings – and this is true of the earlier houses as much as the later buildings – it is more or less impossible to describe them as incorporating a real distinction between inside and outside. In the case of Frank Gehry, in particular the recent museums, the innovation on the level of form creates a literal surface. In this instance the opposite is the case. The surface, the place of innovation stands in opposition to the depth occurring behind or within it. The surface covers. Consequently, with Gehry's recent work – particularly the Guggenheim Museum Bilbao – the interpretive question concerns the relationship between the surface and the interior. Questioning would necessitate holding to a distinction between the inside and the outside. Not only is there a literal outside, the logic of the building – its operative economy – yields an outside. Excluded from consideration is the possibility of a surface with depth. Eisenman's work, from the use of axonometrics in the design of the Houses to the fold in Rebstockpark, or to the moiré pattern in the Nordliches Derendorf Master Plan Competition, are all intended to displace the oppositions inside/outside or figure/ground. While these oppositions are to a certain extent different what they both intend to establish is a juxtaposition that defines the space of the architectural as opposed to its setting. They seek to establish an-other than architecture as part of a set up in which the architectural is given as being in opposition to its other. Overcoming the hold of these oppositions occurs neither by destruction nor forgetting but by the introduction of the unpredictable. Again, it is essential to note that it is not unpredictability *tout court*, but one both defined in relation to function and only possible because the enacted retention of function.

The production of the unpredictable is a fundamental element in the majority of the projects. Unpredictability is defined as a complex point of intersection. It occurs at the point created by the interconnection of the experiential and the formal thereby reinforcing the points of connection between the early House projects and the more recent urban projects. Writing of House III Eisenman describes the relationship between occupant and house in the following terms;

> In the process of taking possession the owner begins to destroy; albeit in a positive sense, the initial unity and completeness of the architectural structure. ... By acting in response to a given structure, the owner is now almost working against this pattern. By working to come to terms with this structure, design is not decoration but rather becomes a process of inquiry into one's own latent capacity to understand any man-made space.[6]

It would be incorrect to argue that the disjunction between the owner and structure gives the latter a purely formal and thus an internally regulated economy. Such a position would fail to recognize that House III works in its own specific way within the opening given by the logic of the apart/a part in which what is already at hand – given within repetition, though given to be transformed – is the history of housing and thus the larger history of architecture's relation to the history of domesticity. While it is always the case that this interconnection is present with any house, merely operating on that level is to insist on continuity. As the possibility of discontinuity depends upon continuity – the 'apart' depends upon the presence of the 'a part' – what has to emerge is an experiential engagement with the presence of that history. However, the engagement will involve a transformation of some of the constitutive elements of that history. Experience needs to be understood therefore as already staged within dominant structures whose repetition is the work and practice both of history and the everyday. An intervention into that set up, described above as that which causes the owner to have to work, necessitates the engendering of experiential possibilities. Experience is denied its merely phenomenological form on the one hand, while on the other, the possibility that sustains and opens up the world of experience, reviving the deadening of experience that forms an integral part of modernity, is neither mere shock nor carnival but the work of the house itself.

The recent urban projects for Frankfurt and Dusseldorf are initially able to bear a neo-formalist interpretation insofar as they could be understood as engaging with the problem of the generation of site. The moiré pattern, catastrophe theory or the fold produce the site. Nonetheless what is guiding the folding, or the use of the moiré is the attempt to establish a deformation that refers continually to the history and urban planning of the site in question. The ascription of formalism therefore would be inaccurate. Here, there is an important analogy with Eisenman's own description of the logic governing House III. In its clear link to experience, the programmatic and the formal intention at work within the House already works to acknowledge the inscription – understood in terms of experience – of the history of housing. A similar movement is also operative within the urban projects. While the particularity of each of the projects is different the specific is itself established by the retention of a strong relationship between the design process and the historical determinations that are already given with the nature of the generic possibility to be repeated.

In another recent urban project – the Bahnhofbereich Freidrichstrasse Competition – the designation of the site within the Office's own project description reinforces the way the centrality of function – the creation of an urban setting – utilizes the given in order to transform that which is given. What is given is retained but only in its being transformed. Once more this movement is only really adequately explicable in terms of the logic of the apart/a part: 'the object attempts to produce a multilayered superimposition of the histories of Berlin, transforming them into a dynamic model for twenty-first century urbanism'. There is a similar formulation within Rebstock Master Plan. In that case the utilization of the fold was 'to initiate new social organization of social space'. What both projects demonstrate therefore is that the creation of the site and thus the utilization of an experimental procedure was thought within the twofold impossibility of destruction and the utopian. To give this set up a positive or affirmative description it could be argued that the incorporation of the complex experiments aimed to generate the sites are conditioned – and here it is tempting to add exclusively conditioned – by the retention of a function which, in being retained is transformed. Rephrasing this it could be suggested that what is involved are architectural or urban undertakings that admitted the ubiquity of repetition and thus the need to engage with the given but which identified an opening defying the work of prediction. Such openings would stem from and thus be positioned by the work of the logic of the apart/a part. Again what is fundamental is an experience of a particular determination of the incomplete. There is a further sense of the incomplete. Here it emerges in the way in which the building interacts with the preexisting structures. The buildings create spaces as a consequence of their relationship. Domains awaiting programme are the consequence of allowing two different design process to interconnect. Nonetheless, the to-be-programmed quality is not open ended. It is conditioned by the possible programmes that can incorporated into a school of architecture, design and art. Moreover this quality of the yet-to-be is interconnected with a general sense of the incomplete that works within the experiential hold of the structure. What the building causes the occupant to act out is the affirmation of a lack of mastery. The impact of the building is at its most demanding when the desire within design has to yield, cede place to an adventure that has to oscillate between the pragmatic, to be understood as the necessity to decide, and the impossibility of linking that decision to a completing finality. It is in these terms that it holds to the presence of a productive negativity. The lesson of the building lies in its didactic quality. What is significant however is that that quality is not a nihilistic didacticism refusing the didactic, nor is the didactic quality one that imposes a certain procedure to be followed. The building works by upsetting that possibility. The building's singularity lies in its refusal to impart a mimetic impulse, while at the same time working within the constraint of having to allow for design. In other words, its singularity is given by the work of the logic of the apart/a part. The didactic quality is the complex relation that any occupant – student/professor/visitor – has to have with its insistent singularity. What makes the quality insistent is that it arises from holding to the strong relationship between form and function and suspending the possibility of critical ambivalence by the inscription of an inbuilt futurity. The transformation of the nature of that relationship which occurs by linking it to the presence of a productive negativity and the work of the logic of the apart/a part does nor efface the relationship. Rather it is retained as present, even though it is a presence that is mediated by the ineliminable work of the incomplete.

Finally, the presence of an in built futurity is only explicable in terms of allowing for the presence of function – thus a functioning building – that eschews the self-identical precisely because it refuses the original unity of function. In the place of ambivalence there would be a recasting of function. Moreover, it would be an architectural

3

OPENING RESISTING FORMS

RECENT PROJECTS OF REISER AND UMEMOTO

OPENING

The architectural practice of Reiser and Umemoto has a direct impact upon architectural theory.[1] And yet theirs is not a theoretical architecture. Rather, their own important innovations within architecture demand that particular response from architectural theory in which the theoretical must continually invent in order to respond to the insistence of their work. Work sets the measure for theory. In taking up the four projects – Yokohama Port Terminal, Cardiff Bay Opera House, Kansai Library, Bucharest 2000 – a sustained attempt has been made to stay with the projects themselves. These projects are situated at a vital moment within the development of the practice and the theory of architecture. In regards to practice it is not just the specific use made of technological innovations that is fundamental, technology has provided the models in terms of which these innovations are to be understood, and, just as significantly, the computer has become a device that is inseparable from the design process itself. The development of complex surfaces, the shifts in how topology operates have become the work of animation and computer generation. Part of what marks out the significance of Reiser and Umemoto's work is that the engagement with the development of topology has not become an end itself. In eschewing a certain formalism they have developed projects that open up the possibility of architectural interventions that resist a celebration of a simple novelty on the one hand and didacticism on the other.

The full force of their work demands a larger setting. What has to be outlined is a context. The generality in question necessitates an identification of the contemporary in architecture. Within this setting it can be argued that there are, in their different forms, two concerns that mark the practice of architecture at the present. These concerns inevitably show themselves in different ways and with different results. In the first place there is the possibility of avoiding the trap of mere novelty while still producing an architecture that is marked by its own version of alterity; an otherness that defies an immediate reduction to a dominant tradition. (In the end these concerns will need to be formulated in terms of a complex structure of repetition.)[2] It is clear, of course, that there can always be a negative response to the question of alterity. Within it, conventions would be celebrated for their own sake and architecture would slide inexorably into building. Concerns with elegance and beauty intermingled with what would emerge as a spurious conception of safety would take the place of an affirmation of alterity and distance. And yet, because the inscription of alterity is neither automatic nor straightforwardly programmatic, what this means is that strategies marking out the process of alterity and distance need to be taken up with great care.[3]

The second concern pertains to what might be described as the problem of formalism. (A problem that can only be dealt with here in outline.) It is not as though architecture can escape a type of formalism. In the design process – e.g. the move from plan to section – there is a necessary and obvious formal dimension. Here, formalism presents itself in a different way and brings with it a different quality. The problem of formalism can be defined as emerging at that moment in a work in which formal innovation, and thus possible alterity, is promulgated in a way that intends to be indifferent to function.[4] Function is introduced but only as a predicate to an already formally construed subject. It is by tracing some of these concerns and their concurrent connection to the question of alterity that it becomes possible to approach the recent work of Reiser and Umemoto. In order to take up that work it is essential to develop these opening considerations. Such a move needs to work through the projects. However, prior to that it is equally important to give what will be the register of their work a setting. In other words, further consideration must be given to the setting of architecture.

BUILDING ACTIVITY

Apart from itself what does architecture stage? Starting with a question, means that a beginning can be made with a complex series of possibilities. The question, while allowing for a certain innocence – the presence of a question demanding an answer – is always more demanding than it seems. In the first place, that demand hinges on the word 'stage'. Indeed, this word brings with it the setting in which the complex possibilities involved in the interpretation of architectural practice can be situated. Staging sets in play a number of openings. However, before discussing their important moments of difference and interconnection, it is essential to stay with staging. There is an element within all of these openings that is similar. The similarity is activity. Staging – the staging at work in the question concerning what it is that architecture stages – involves activity, process and movement. Staging announces therefore the presence of an already existing economy; an economy that in opening up yields the presence of differing economies. While it remains the case that activity, movement – thus the presence of economies – all have to admit of the differences that mark important divergences within the interpretation of architectural practice, it is vital, here, to remain with activity.

How then is the activity to be understood? To insist on the presence of activity, of the economic, within architecture, is not to insist on the primacy of construction. Rather, activity is linked to the built. And yet, despite the simplicity of this formulation it brings with it a complicating factor. As will emerge in greater detail in the argument to come; the built can only be understood with reference to time. Time inheres in building in different ways. (This set up – *built time* – is discussed in detail in the analyses to come.) Built time is always present in terms of the way modalities of completion work within the building's own economy. Or, more specifically, it will be effective, at work, within the way certain conceptions – differing and perhaps incompatible conceptions – of historical time are operative within the structuration of different buildings. Regardless of the construal that time comes to be given, it will have already been at work in the work of architecture. Working with the assumption that time is only present in its already having been located in particular determinations – e.g. narrative time, filmic time, – what marks out this project is that it starts with the recognition of the already connected presence of activity, architecture and time. These terms therefore – *activity, built time* –

are not only interarticulated, both their generality, that which is under discussion in this instance, as well as their particularity, that which will be taken up within a consideration of specific projects, open up the staging of architecture.

Activity becomes a way of describing both the presence of a building as well as the presence of an urban field. However, what does it mean to describe a building as active, as having activity and thus as having its own economy? In general terms, the answer to this question is best provided by beginning with that which stands opposed to activity namely the static, or the fixed. While the opposition should not be taken as straightforward, existing thereby as a simple either/or, it is nonetheless the case that the point of the contrast is between construing the object – the building, the urban field – in terms of, either, a dynamic process in which the object is taken as enacting, thus staging, its own project, or as given by a complete and self-present finality. In the latter case – the assumption of fixity – the object's meaning is the locus of investigation. This occurs in the place of any concentration on the way form and function are interarticulated (their interarticulation entails that design becomes inseparable from function and thus programmatic considerations.) Meaning locates the building within the domain of the visual, while process identifies the building's work as the work of architecture. In sum, with the assumption of fixity the object is taken as a given and as such an analysis of it becomes a description of the given, with the possible concomitant attempt to attribute a specific meaning to the object. In the case of the former – object as dynamic process – the object is attributed a project that it, as an object, seeks to realize. The object has a self-effecting presence; it seeks to realize itself. Effectuation is the movement involved. The utilization of an expression such as 'seeks to realize' is intended to underscore the centrality of activity. Defining both activity and move- ment in relation to the object's work and thus as internal to the object is intended to reinforce the attribution of an economy to the object, and thus to define the object in terms of an ontology of becoming.

Here, it is essential to be precise concerning what is meant by the object. There are two elements involved in the answer to this ques- tion. In the first place, there is the specific architectural or urban object under consideration. In the second, there is the more exacting problem of how its being as an object is to be understood. It is in terms of this second consideration that activity, and built time, need to be positioned. As will become clear, however, the second comes to be read back into the first; i.e. back through and thus into the particular object. The capacity for its being able to be read back in entails that it was already a part of the particular object. Indeed, in a sense, it will have already been central to any investigation of the object's particularity.

What is being addressed in the second is the ontology of the object. It goes without saying that pragmatically what is under consideration is, for example, a specific building; a building which can be located within a given historical frame and to which functional and program-matic concerns can be attributed. While it is always possible both to interpret a given building in different ways, and, to attribute a range of differing symbolic meanings to it, it remains the case that in the act of interpretation, and in the attribution of a certain symbolic force, the ontology of the object – here the building – is only ever addressed tangentially. Meaning is privileged and thus the specificity of the archi-tectural object – the being of the object *qua* object – remains unaddressed. Architecture is reduced therefore to the symbolic pres-ence of the object.[5] There is no suggestion here that a building or urban condition do not have or should not have a symbolic dimen-sion. All that is being questioned is the identification of architecture with the building's symbolic register. In sum, the symbolic is equated with the ontological. (The existence of the object is its existence as a symbol.) The question is therefore, what is involved in addressing the ontological directly? There has already been a preliminary attempt to answer this question. What has to be recognized is that the contrast between the static and the fixed on one side, and process and becoming on the other, should not be understood as a simple choice; a choice with the same ontological setting. The difference cannot be thought therefore in terms of variety. Moreover, it cannot be understood as allowing for a form of reduction in which the elements comprising the differences could themselves be explicated in terms of a founding unity. The distinction has to be understood as ontological in nature. What this entails is that the distinction – a difference resisting reduc-tion – has to be described in terms of a differential ontology. In other words, it is a distinction concerning two different, and in the end irre-ducible, ways of explicating the differing modes of being proper to the object – here the building.

Stasis and becoming do not comprise a divide that separates build-ings and urban fields. They mark out the presence of different ways of construing what is ostensibly the 'same' object. It is only within the construal itself that it becomes possible to generate differences between types of architectural practice. The force of the difference lies in the way time figures within the way the object comes to be formulated.

Once activity is taken as central and the object explained in terms of its attempt to realize its own project, then, not only does this eliminate the intrusion of a new formalism, this elimination becomes a necessary consequence of inscribing function as central to the object. Function is, after all, what the building seeks to realize. Arguing against this position would have to assume the viability of the proposition that architecture could create a value free and hence neutral space that simply awaited functional or programmatic considerations. As will emerge from the work under consideration here not only is that impossible, the real force of the capacity of the yet-to-be, what will be developed here in outline in terms of the incomplete, only emerges when it is indissolubly linked to functional concerns. To the extent that functional concerns are taken as central to any consideration of the object – again function as an integral part of the object's self-effectuation – this will have two important consequences. The first will be an opening up of function. The second concerns activity and the building's economy. It is linked to the first, however it brings with it the complex interconnection between function and design.

The interconnection has two significant elements. On the one hand, once function is understood as always already integral to the design process then any engagement with function will have to bring with it an engagement with design. And yet, on the other hand, there is also the important corollary, that a simple change on the level of design does not entail an examination let alone a shift in how function is understood and is thus present. In other words, if there is an engagement with function then that has design implications. However, innovation on the level of design may leave function unaddressed. This latter possibility almost inevitably arises from the situation in which design is thought not to have direct functional implications.[6]

There is an inevitable risk in using a term such as function. It is often taken as unidimensional. The break with function therefore is thought to be a break with function itself when in fact such a conception of the break positions function as unidimensional in order then that the break be effected. Not only is this to fail to understand the

nature of function, such a position often brings with it, as has been
intimated, a commitment, no matter how implicitly stated, of a space
independent of functional and programmatic considerations. Because
of the complexity and the difficulty of this position it is vital to move
slowly. Function is not given within an either/or (either there is the
function or there is the appearance of the functionally neutral.)
Moreover, the imposition of function, is inescapable. There are two
questions here: What is meant by the presence of the inescapable?
What occurs in the break from a unidimensional conception of function? The key to both these questions is repetition.

Within any designed space, there may be space awaiting the injection of programme; and therefore such a space must have the status
of the yet-to-be programmed. Within any designated building the functional may not have an exact relation to design. In the slippage there
may be functional concerns that are also marked by this yet-to-be.
However, the setting in which these futural projections occur is the
object itself. In other words, the future is conditioned by the nature
of the present. Moreover, it is conditioned by the retention, the necessary retention, of the function that the building seeks to realize. It is
thus that there is an inescapability of function. Furthermore, what
makes functional concerns inescapable is that function is already
specific. There are in fact only functions; functions which are repeated
within any new instance of a specific and thus functional building.
What is repeated is not the unidimensional nature of function but the
dominant conception that a particular function has and thus the way
in which the design process must allow for the relatively unproblematic repetition of that function.

The inescapable therefore is the inescapability of repetition. The
apparent unidimensionality of function is simply that interarticulation
of design and function enabling the repetition of dominance. Once the
object is construed in terms of activity then the logic of the building
– the building's own economy – concerns the nature of its relationship to repetition. The inescapability of repetition generates both a site
of judgement and the locus of intervention. It is in terms of this setting
that invention needs to be positioned. Invention cannot be disassoci-
ated from the work of repetition. Even if there are only functions,
even within a delineated function – e.g. a library – there is both a
possible repetition of dominance, the dominant configuration of technology, power and knowledge, or a repetition in which the function

of the library is only held in place to the extent that the function is transformed. The transformation is effected by design but is only successful because of the secured centrality of a function to be transformed. Intervention and invention combine in that they become repetition's other possibility. Detailing this position means linking it to what has already been identified as built time.

DEVELOPING BUILT TIME

Writing of a specific project – his own design for the Cardiff Bay Opera House – Greg Lynn reformulated what he identifies as 'novelty' in the following terms,

> Novelty, rather than an extrinsic effect, can be conceived as the catalyst of new and *unforeseeable* organizations that proceed from the interaction between freely differentiating systems and their incorporation of external constraints.[7] (My emphasis.)

While it will always be essential to return to the detail of this claim, its initial importance is its location of that which is yet to be seen. Even though it can be attributed generality insofar as his argument could also concern the interaction of general systems or the interaction of systems removed from the particularity of a specific object, it has additional purchase when it comes to the description of particularity, since it can be further argued that what he identifies as 'interaction' could in fact be a description of the generation of particularity itself. There is no reason to believe that particularity cannot pertain either to the building or to the urban field.

Part of the force of this description is that it brings the future, here identified as the 'unforeseeable', into play. There is an inscription of the future. However, it is not an inscription that is in any way futural, if the future is merely a posited and often utopian counter to the present. Lynn's argument involves the inscription of the future within the present. In this instance the future occurs and is thus present within the organization of the present. Once the future becomes a condition of the present, then the present becomes a complex and irreducible site. The present resists the possibility of its being present to itself. It is, of course, in terms of the future that it is possible to differentiate between conceptions of activity. Moreover, the inscription of the future

– the yet-to-be – marks the presence of a different economy than one
concerned to close down the future or to give it a precise determination in terms of reuse. The inherent conceptual difficulty of this
position, at this stage, must be allowed to endure.

A similar temporal organization is evident in John Rajchman's engagement with the question of the new within architecture. Addressing
this question he argues that

> the avant-garde wished to resolve the tension between art and
> technological necessity by displaying 'function' in visible form,
> rather than trying to expose in given forms the tension with func-
> tion that is the chance of the *invention to come*. (My emphasis.)

For Rajchman the limit of what he identifies as the 'avant-garde' is
that its project works by closing the temporal gap between form and
function such that one is incorporated within the other. It is as though
form becomes the representation of function. Here, completion is not
simply a structural question it is equally a temporal one. However,
there are two different temporalities at stake. In contradistinction to
the temporal closure – a set up that demands the excision of deferral
and thus a relation of immediacy between form and function – there
is a time that works between immediate closure and pure openness.

In working between them it becomes a conception of temporality
that resists the opposition between closure and openness. As such
rather than demanding that the presence of one exclude the other they
become copresent – co-present in their difference – within the object.
Indeed it will be in terms of their copresence that the opposition comes
to be transformed. In the place of an excluding opposition between
closure and openness there is the productive interplay of the complete
and the incomplete. Both terms designate different ways in which
design and function are interarticulated.[8]

What this entails is that an opening emerges which is other than a
simple middle point. The relation involves greater complexity. Indeed,
it is that complex relation between architecture and time that insists
within Rajchman's formulation of an 'invention to come' or in what
Lynn identifies by the 'unforeseeable'. What renders these formulations complex is that within them space is either yet to be formed, or
formed as indeterminate. These possibilities, which become the inscription of a temporality of the incomplete into the economy of the

building, are formed within the project such that they work to inform the programme. The importance of Lynn's description of this state of affairs is that his recognition of the importance of constraints and thus the necessity not to accept any one determination of a constraint as a *fait accompli* works to avoid the possibility of a merely formal innovation. This recognition is also at work in Rajchman's formulation. When he links 'invention' to a 'tension with function', then the important question concerns how it is that function is retained within and as part of that site of tension. (They must be thought therefore in terms of the logic of the apart/a part.) While this is a fundamental question, what it retains as its premise, though perhaps, more emphatically, as its condition of possibility, is the further consequence that 'invention' is only possible because of function's retention.

Before turning to the projects themselves it is essential to take up the incomplete. Again, while allowing for the retention of generality, it is essential to reiterate that what is involved here is the incomplete in architecture. Defining it is this way means that the incomplete has to be linked to what has emerged thus far concerning activity and built time. In sum, the incomplete can only be thought in relation to the way repetition works within the production of architecture.

In general terms the incomplete becomes a way of holding to the presence of function whilst at the same time holding open the precise nature and thus the realization of that function. The building becomes an unmasterable site precisely because the already present determinations demanded by the slogan of form follows function have themselves been opened up. Opening up the tight interconnection inherent in that demand yields neither the appearance of neutrality – function as the 'afunctional' – nor the utopian. What emerges is that which will be present in terms of the yet-to-be. However this possibility is, as has already been indicated, the inscription of the future into the present. The unmasterability of that inscription – and it is an inscription realized by the formal practice of architecture – yields the opening that allows for the possibility of alterity in architecture; other times and other buildings.

The incomplete depends up on the complete. The latter is finitude, the former is the potential infinite defined in relation to that finitude. In pragmatic terms the incomplete is an immaterial effect inscribed in the building's work having a material source. Terms such as finite and infinite need to be taken as temporal terms. An architecture that seeks to close down the potential opening and questioning of function achieves this end by attempting to exclude the incomplete and thereby to create a work determined by self-control and self-presence. Mastery excludes the place of a productive opening by its retention of determined prediction; it is retained in the place of chance. Allowing for the incomplete and therefore a retained immaterial presence, is, once more, to allow for alterity and distance within architecture.

YOKOHAMA PORT TERMINAL

Temporal complexity governs the economy of Reiser and Umemoto's Yokohama Port Terminal project. Not only is there the temporality of the incomplete, this is connected to the already present temporal distinction envisaged in the project's use. The passage of ships and the use of the terminal as a port involves a different rhythm than the everyday use of the site occasioned by the presence of gardens and other activity areas. What needs to be pursued is the relation between these differing forms of time. As a preliminary move however the differences between the conventions of shed building need to be distinguished from what was proposed for the port terminal. These two sets of temporal distinctions are interconnected. Difference within programme is sustained by the building's own productive economy. Articulating the difference with shed construction necessitates returning to the productive presence of time; in other words, it demands specifying the way built time can be linked to the incomplete and to that extent enjoins alterity by giving it a formal presence. It should not be thought however that built time is connected only to the incomplete. As will be suggested built time is equally as operative in the claim that the nineteenth century shed is enacted within – and to that extent enacts – a temporality of determined completion. In other words, determined completion is another form of built time.

In their own description of the project Reiser and Umemoto refer to the differing senses of the incomplete operative within the work. What can be taken as incomplete is present in both in the concept governing the project and in the way the envisaged structure would work to enact it.[9] In regards to the latter their position is articulated in relation to the tradition of shed building. What guides that tradition is the creation of uniformity. The structure would have to sustain

Figure 3.1   Yokohama port terminal: view of terminal pier

and maintain a spatial dimension that admitted of only one determination. As homogeneity should not just be a description of the space, but also has to be maintained by the work of the overall structure, such that framing works to create a space articulating a repetition of the Same. Within this particular repetition – and it is clear that it is a repetition that is structural as much as it is conceptual – built time is presented as both totality and finality. Homogeneity, while spatial, admits of a temporal description insofar as what marks out the nineteenth century shed is the interplay between spatial homogeneity and temporal finality. The importance of insisting on this interplay is that it produces the site in which it becomes possible to position distancing as yielding the place of alterity. In other words, it yields the site of both intervention and invention.

Countering this conception of built time could be envisaged as dividing up the internal area in such way that an apparent complexity would have been introduced. However, the complexity in question would have been simply quantitative in nature. It would be as though

Figure 3.2   Yokohama port terminal: view of underside of roof

the greater the divisions within a single space, then the greater the degree of complexity. Not only does such a position misconstrue the nature of complexity, it entails, in the end that complexity be nor more than a form of confusion. The question, therefore, is what is involved in the introduction of complexity once it is no longer understood as quantitative in nature?

Answering this question on a general level is to assert first that complexity is only possible once there is a founding irreducibility; and secondly where the irreducible is explicable in ontological and temporal terms. As such the mark of a complex would be the copresence of the complete and the incomplete or the material and the immaterial. Complexity becomes the affirmed presence of a plural event.[10] The difficulty is, that as this is not a theoretical or general claim that can only be instantiated in one specific form, then the move to the specific has to hold to the insistence of particularity. In fact, particularity can be defined as precisely that relation between the plural event and its affirmed specific presence. It is thus that there can be no architecture of the present – as opposed to building – without the event. The nineteenth century shed can be taken as attempting to eliminate the possibility of a founding complexity by eliminating the incomplete. As such particularity would have been effaced by the drive for a repetitive continuity of the self-same. The response to this drive – what would amount to an intervention into this form of repetition – would necessitate a disruption that is the intrusion of other spatial possibilities. Reiser and Umemoto refer to this disruption in terms of 'perturbations' and 'transformations'.

Different forms of development are envisaged within the overall structure. These disruptions are made possible by the initial use of a determined structural model. Rather than an overall homogeneous structure with its own surface – maintaining the received conditions of inside/outside and surface/depth – the incorporation of the possibility of differential growth stemming from the specific use of the three hinged arch allows for mutations that overcome the idea of linear development. Spacing works by working through spaces. Part of the project's own activity is its effecting spacing. This would occur by the way in which the reiteration of the building would, in the addition of further elements, create additional spaces and thus sites within the overall structure which are, of course, envisaged as already being part of the structure. A way of describing this conception of addition would be to formulate it in the following terms: $x + y = x + y + z$. In the case of the tradition of shed building. The addition of 'y' to 'x' would be straightforwardly '$x + y$'. In this instance the addition of 'z' has to be understood as the unpredictable consequence of adding 'y' to 'x'. What will be known henceforth as the 'z factor', is a created space that is always internal to the object. While it is always mediated by the function of the object, it nonetheless opens up programmatic possibilities that cannot have been predicated. Again, this has to be understood as the inscription of the future into the present. Accounting for the 'z factor' has to involve a detailed account of how surfaces contain depths that eschew the automatic functional control of the flat surface. Depth need not be taken literally. It is rather that depth, in this instance, attests to the presence of a complex surface and therefore needs to be understood as an important development within topology.

In this specific case this system also works both to integrate the two elements of the building – port and community space – while simultaneously holding them apart. Moreover the generation a surface that is not just the roof, but a roof having its own depth and thus a differential structure that is itself self-generated by the process that yields part of the interior space, allows for different permutations of the surface and thus of its possible use.

The important element is that the reiteration of the frame – a reiteration generating and inscribing difference – allows the structure to work by distancing the hold of a simple syntax by yielding areas and thus spaces that work to determine the nature of the programme specifically because they can be described as the 'unforeseeable organizations' whose use and thus whose function always has to be negotiated. The presence of the yet-to-be in this instance would be generated by the building's own self-realization and thus would be integral to its operation and thus activity as a building. (Again, what has to be noted is the interplay of activity and built time.) The economy in question has inscribed the possibility of an 'invention to come' within its own practice. What emerges therefore is an opening for building that demands its own theoretical response. Demands are made once the site of repetition demands another form – and almost invariably this will be a productive form – of iterative activity.

First, therefore what occurs with this project can in the first instance be defined negatively. There is neither a repetition of a specific tradition within architecture, nor is there a purely speculative and utopian gesture. Second, there is the affirmative description. Guiding this description is the irruption of the unpredictable from that which is already present within architecture. There needs to be a different form of repetition. This repetition is not the presence of a ghost haunting the architectural nor is it merely the recognition of the uncanny – the uncanny, after all leaves the initial house intact. There must be a twofold movement that is both an extrusion and intrusion. It is this state of affairs that is identified by Stan Allen in terms of the task '... to define a sustainable project of creative work, capable of perturbing existing categories by the production of something unrecognisable out of that which is all too familiar.'[11]

The negative and the positive description are imbricated. What is created by their overlap is the space to come in the precise sense that it is the space which is already there. This affirmation of the presence of the future within the present is one of the dominant motifs of Reiser and Umemoto's architectural projects. Indeed, it is that which works define the operation of built time in their projects.

CARDIFF BAY OPERA HOUSE

This project concerns the event of architecture. Not the event of a building, but a building as an occurrence within the urban fabric. In other words, what determines this project is a refusal to position the building as independent of its setting. And yet, on the other hand, it cannot be suggested that the project is driven by a simple contextualism. It is rather that what allows for the positioning of the Opera House is the attribution of a quality in which it forms part of the infra-structure of the Cardiff Bay area. What this means is initially difficult to explicate and therefore it is easier to define the project in the negative. Initially, what this positioning entails is that instead of viewing the building as self-enclosed and therefore only present in term of its relation to its own context, the building takes on the quality of the context, thereby transforming what is meant by context. (It is this twofold movement involving transformation that is part of what marks out the power of this project.) While specificity is held in place – it remains an opera house – the question of how it relates to its context is resisted by its lack of indifference to its context. As they indicate in their own project notes, Reiser and Umemoto understand this play with context as a way of avoiding positing a singular building that would then become a separate and individuated cultural monument. (As will be seen this link to the problem of the monument is also central to their conception of the Bucharest 2000 project.)

There are two aspects of this project that need to be pursued. The first is the detail of how the building works as infrastructure. The second is the way this happens as a direct result of the building's design. These two elements are related since it is the use of what they call a 'geodetic bag' that enables the first to work. In their own description of the geodetic they note that,

> In an architectural context ... with the interest in structural systems that could engender complexity through flexibility, geodetics becomes interesting precisely because as a system, it is capable of adapting to complex spatial formations without a corresponding increase in the complexity of the system.[12]

While it may be necessary to equivocate over the use of the word complexity since 'complexity of the system' may involve a different sense of complexity than the one engendered 'through flexibility', it remains the case that what this formulation envisages is a geometry that enables, in this instance, a series of relations between the inside and the outside, and between different parts of the building, that are both absolute yet porous. Programmatic specificity is maintained despite the centrality of movement defining occupation and thus experience within the building. This provides a way of beginning to understand they way in which the building inscribes and to that extent repeats the set up proper to infrastructure rather than the set up proper to the isolated, and therefore isolating, cultural monument.

The consequence of the use of a geodetic structural system is that it is able to bear different elements and thus provide different surface effects. It is this provision that reworks the oppositions inside/outside and separate/combined. In, for example, the envisaged concourse and foyer area the capacity of the surface to bear difference while remaining structurally the same means that it would be possible to allow for a continuity between foyer and auditorium without that continuity having a determining impact on the different programmatic demands specific to each. Entry into the building from the piazza then to concourse, foyer and auditorium is smooth despite the insistence of programmatic differences. Again, this is the effect of the capacity of the geodetic structure to bear differences. However what is essential is the contrast. In other words, it is important to show what is being resisted with this structure.

While it is difficult to generalize it is nonetheless possible to envisage an opera house in which entry from the street led directly into a foyer. The foyer opened to a service area with drink and food provision which in turn led to the auditorium. This structure might vary on each floor – for example the upper floor concourse areas might lead directly into the auditorium – nonetheless what would characterize such a set up would be the necessity of a complete division between the different areas, and, where the divisions within the building bore a more or less direct relationship to the geometry of the building. The separation of the different programmatic elements within the building would work to establish the presence of the building as singular and therefore as a potential monument. In addition, its internal divisions and thus its potential separateness would demand that it be viewed not as infrastructure but as existing in relation to a context. It would be in that relation that its potential monumentality would be realized.

It is vital to note that what enables the distancing of this set up is neither a different conception of programming nor the intrusion of other ways of construing division within an already existing building form. What marks out their project is that the inscription of difference is an effect of the geometry. Tracing the work of the 'geodetic bag' through the exterior to the interior would be to follow the unfolding of a single surface which was able to generate differences. The creation of divisions that were neither open nor closed, positionings that were neither inside nor outside except at the extreme, are not the work of internal construction and thus the necessary effect of partitioning. This set up is the creation – thus the effect – of a complex surface. It is the surface effect generating programmatic possibilities. As has already been intimated, positioning the building as a series of openings in which movement into it, through it and within it, defined, and in a certain sense generated, the building, works to rob it of the possibility of monumentality. This is not loss but a redefinition that occurs because these openings define the building as part of the activity that defines the urban setting. Access brings with it the flows and holds of the setting itself. This has the further effect of allowing the retention of functional specificity; the building works as an opera house, the complexity of the rehearsal hall further opens up a range of possible *theatrical* forms. However function is retained beyond the hold of a certain conception of culture due to the integration of the building into a field of activity. It would have been integrated into it without being the same as it. This is a direct consequence of a project that takes movement and activity as its point of departure.

KANSAI LIBRARY

How, today, is a library to be designed? What, today, is a library? While these questions can always be made more specific insofar as the type of library can be specified; the setting can be delineated; its relation to an already existing public as opposed to a private domain of activity can be adumbrated; it remains the case that with the question of the library there is a set up in which the concerns of the present already confront the complex relationship between technology and the storage and utilization of knowledge. The library become the stage on which the relationship between knowledge and power is enacted with a singular force within this moment of modernity's unfolding. What then of the library? Answering this question entails identifying what is specific about the Kansai Library project. It is the envisaged building's particularity that sets the stage for a return to the more general question of the library.

There are two interrelated strategies that can be identified in this particular project. The first involves the problem of storage and access. The second is the way that activity occurs within the library. Perhaps the most dramatic, and yet also the most simple, transformation that occurs in their project is the separation of these domains. The storage unit for books and documents occurs in a building structured around efficient storage. Here efficiency is not the existence of an archive resisting access. What is vital to the Stack Building is ease of the entry of material into the storage area and then the capacity to deploy those materials within the library building itself.

The usual dilemma confronting the library concerns how to incorporate storage and public use within one building. Here it has been solved by having two buildings connected by an automated conveyor system. (Movement between the building is equally as important as movement within the library building itself. Movement in the work of the project is productive.) While there are materials housed in the actual library building its importance as a building emerges in its have

Figure 3.3
Kansai Library:
interior
perspective

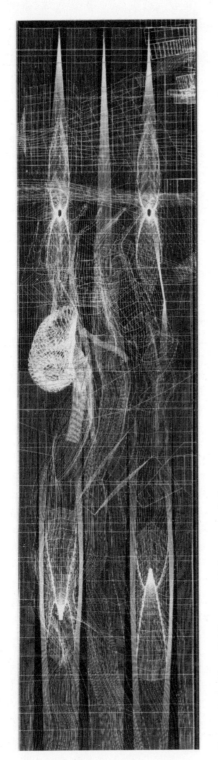

Figure 3.4 Kansai Library: wideframe roof plan

Figure 3.5   Kansai Library: 2nd floor plan

been freed from the major problems of storage. As such, the question that arises concerns its activity as a building. Taking up this question brings design and function into connection. In order to emphasize the consequence of their design it is helpful to contrast the building with a three story library in which the floors consisted of distinct, unidimensional slabs and in which the connection between the floors consisted of a public staircase and a semi-public elevator. While each floor could carry different programmatic possibilities, the system governing a particular possibility on the first floor could not, by definition, interconnect with a different system on another floor. The only way it would be possible to define a relationship between the floor slabs would be in terms of the stair case or the elevator. The interconnection would be between modes of access and the floors themselves. In other words, what comes to be precluded is the possible interconnection of what has already been identified as the 'interaction' of different systems. What guides Reiser and Umemoto's approach is that they wish to allow for this form of connection with the consequence that the relationship between domains of the library would be brought about with the result of producing the unforeseen. In other words, of structuring the design process such that it is driven by the possible irruption, and hence interruption, of the 'z factor'.

Figure 3.6 Kansai Library: perspective of exterior

It is this possibility that defines the way in which the internal operation of the library building would work. Instead of floors that are
necessarily discreet there is an envisaged ramp system. The use of such
a system redefines the spatial configurations across the ramp, the movement up and down the ramp and, from differing positions, one slab
in relation to another. As with the Yokohama project what allows for
these reworked relations is the way in which the ramps function as a
surface. What is excluded is unidimensionality. The difficult problem
is trying to describe the differing ways in which it is excluded.

The use of a geodetic structure would allow the ramps to be
suspended. They are cut by vertical as well as horizontal modes of
access. (It must be admitted however that with a ramp system which
in some sense generates a continuous surface, any straightforward
conception of horizontality becomes problematic.) However, rather
than the more conventional entry via either a stairwell or an elevator,
differing points of entry allow the relationship between access and the
place of access to become differing intersections with differing programmatic possibilities. The point of orientation has to start with the surface.

The floor space within a three story building with a unidimensional
surface would only allow for differing programmatic possibilities that
are given through addition and division. The area can be divided and

the configuration of public and private space only changed with addition of either temporary or permanent dividing walls. All such conceptions of change have to accept the building as complete; thus it is this overriding sense of containment the delimits the range of the possible. In a general sense this is the surface effect of a what has already been described as a unidimensional surface. Moreover, in such a building there would be three different floor surfaces. (And yet, of course, while being different, it would be a difference defined and delimited by the work of the same.) It is precisely this possibility that the ramp, which can be construed as continuous, resists, and, in resisting it, the way of working within the library comes to be transformed. An occurrence taking place on the level of building – the activity of the building – rather than on the level of meaning. Meaning emerges as a consequence of activity since the transformation have to do with the possibility that chance and the deferral of system would play an important role in how the relationship between technology, power and knowledge is understood. The plan for the Kansai Library project presents such a set up. It would not symbolize it. Rather, a possibility of this type is at work in the building's envisaged structuration and thus in what would emerge as its economy.

The importance of a surface that resists the programmatic determinations stemming from the unidimensional is that rather than blurring distinctions between programmed areas it allows their intersection to open up programmatic possibilities. This has to be understood as another version of the 'z factor'. If x and y are two programmatic possibilities with their own surface relations then allowing for an surface structured by topological deformations is to allow for the overlap of x and y, an overlap generated by the surface itself and in which z is the consequence. It is not the consequence, necessarily, of blurred relations but of overlapping determinations. The overlap is not indifferent to the surface and therefore it is not indifferent to design. It is a consequence of the design itself and therefore part of the surface effect (a position which is the surface's effect). The emergence of the 'z factor' becomes the affirmation of a form of irreducibility. Once again, what this means is that the formula of $x + y = x + y + z$ takes on the status of a plural event. $x + y + z$ is set up that cannot be reduced to its constituent parts. It is therefore the mark of a founding irreducibility that has to be construed as productive and to that extent as a performative.

Finally, therefore, it is the consequence of this formulation that needs to be noted. The question of its import has to be posed in relation to the library. The contrast has already been drawn between two different types of structure. One marked by a series of unidimensional floor slaps and the other by utilizing a continuous complex surface in order to generate unpredictable configurations. While this is a real distinction it remains merely formal unless the constraint of the library is introduced. Once that constraint is allowed to bear on the question of form, then, not only is there the emergence of a different architectural configuration, it will also be the case that that difference intrudes into how the activity of research, the production of knowledge and the public/private distinction occurring within the institutionalization of knowledge, take place.

The site of innovation and intervention occurs to the extent that the presence of the library is held in place. However, the contrast is not between already determined conceptions of the library. The contrast is between a conception of finitude, and thus an architecture of the complete, on the one hand and an inscribed openness dependent upon the interrelationship between the complete and the incomplete on the other. The presence of the incomplete is always marked by the immaterial because it is the presence of the future – the continual opening up of the future – within the present. Again it is essential to be clear. The future in question is not the utopian other. The future is defined by the continual possibility of further 'unforeseen' functional and programmatic determinations sanctioned, in the instance, by the surface effect effecting the work of the incomplete. What this entails is that rather than assuming that the interplay of knowledge and power can only have one determined form – a form governed by a conception of totality in which each move is only ever an element of the totality – there can be the housed presence of the continual possibility, perhaps need, for inventions resisting absorption. This latter possibility is precisely what this conception of the Kansai Library is constrained to allow.

BUCHAREST 2000

Here, context is all. Not the 'provincial contextualism' which Reiser and Umemoto are right to dismiss in their own project description. But the context the awaits what they describe as the 'powerful forces

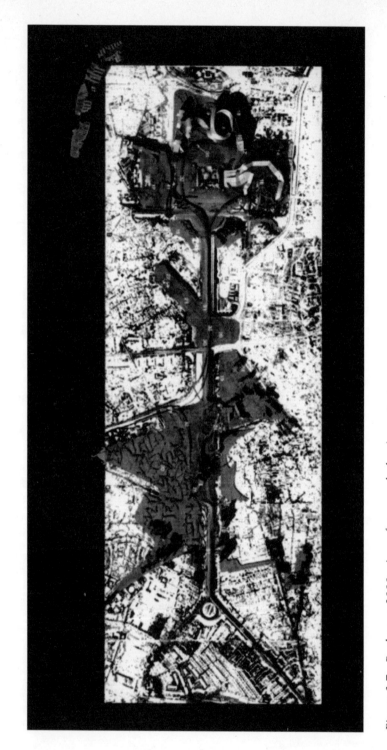

Figure 3.7 Bucharest 2000: view of proposal plan in context

Figure 3.8 Bucharest 2000: plan of proposal

of cultural and economic transformation engendered by a cosmopoli-
tanizing infrastructure.' There cannot be any straightforward escape
from the urban and architectural legacy of Ceaucescu's regime. It is,
of course, the impossibility of escape that must be understood as central
in this context. How, given what Reiser and Umemoto succinctly identify as 'an inflated monumental urbanism' is it possible for there to
be another architecture and thus another urbanism? These demands
gesturing as they do to the problem of the other – another urbanism,
another architecture – raise the important question of what counts as
alterity within the architectural. It should not be forgotten that allowing
for a date to have a determining role – here the year 2000 – introduces another aspect of otherness and another timing manoeuvre
neither of which can be reduced to the simple operation of chronology.
Alterity cannot be taken *in vacuo*, on the contrary, it necessitates its
own context. In this instance the context is given twice. In the first
instance it is Bucharest, in the second it is the presence of a monumental urbanism. It is this doubled context that generates the site.
Moreover it provides the orientation of Reiser and Umemoto's intervention. Theirs is an intervention within this site.

Again it is possible to begin with a question. It is a question that
summarizes the problem of alterity but which recognizes the insistence
of the context; the context as twice given. The question is stark: how
not to continue? Answering this question must begin with what has
already been given. Not only is there a given urban and architectural
set up; such a set up is necessarily overdetermined. Responding must
engage both with the empirical presence of what is there, as well as
its overdetermined nature. What makes it overdetermined in this
context is that both the urban setting and its related buildings already
have a monumental effect. Roads and buildings were intended to function as symbols. As such there is an already present monumentality
carried by the context. Moreover, it is a monumentality that is the
consequence of destruction. Razing the inner city of Bucharest in order
to create a monumental urbanism inscribes destruction at the heart of
the enterprise. Responding to a particular form of destruction cannot
occur as a simple reiteration of that act: a repetition of the Same.
Hence the force of the question: how not to continue?

The project, Bucharest 2000, involves an intervention and transformation of the main area of the city. Not only is there the addition
of infrastructure there is also the introduction of axes through the

Figure 3.9 Bucharest 2000: view of proposal

Figure 3.10 Bucharest 2000: view of northern end of proposal

area; through it thus in part defining it. What guides the addition and the reworking of the road system is what has already been described as the doubled context. A direct way of addressing how an intervention into this site can occur is by starting with the central connecting route Boulevard Unirii.[13] The symbolic importance of this route is clear. It defined a central procession, either to or away from, what had been the Presidential Palace. The route was lined with new apartments blocks, all in a similar style and colour. They provided the perfect corridor down which to approach the Palace. Their uniformity of style helped to control the eye. In fact, it is possible, to argue that the procession and thus the effect created by the approach is structured by an envisaged uniformity of vision. In other words, the urban set up can be understood as involving a twofold relation to sight. In the first instance, it is structured by the uniformity of vision, of what is to be seen. And the second is that it solicits the uniformity of vision, there is only one way of viewing what is to be seen. What the setting demands is a singular gaze. Moreover, it is in terms of this gaze that the monumental effect takes place. Countering an urbanism constructed around this conception of the gaze cannot involve proposing another object, as though the response should be the presence of another object demanding a similar conception of the gaze. In the first instance, the counter move must work within the site and in this sense it must work with the interconnection of movement, vision and the monumental.

The question guiding this analysis – how not to continue? – has to be precise. With what is continuity to be broken? The specification of a site generated by movement, vision and the monumental provides the locus of intervention. Allowing for other possibilities hinges therefore on being able to recast that which generates the site of intervention. In order to realize this possibility a distinction has to be drawn between the anti-monument and the process of demonumentalization. The analogy with myth is important here. If the counter to myth is a generalized demythologization, does that necessitate a counter myth – here that would be the anti-monument – or does it involve a move that demythologizes within a set up that puts the mythic itself into abeyance? It is this latter possibility that is identified above as the process of demonumentalization. Rather than the monument to the end of monuments – or the myth to end all myths – there needs to be another way in. Preliminary to a further investigation of the three elements comprising the site of intervention attention needs to be paid to the consequence of precluding the anti-monument.

Perhaps the most important part of the legacy of Bucharest – a part that cannot be accounted for in any direct manner – is the role of destruction in the creation of the area of the city under consideration. Not continuing cannot escape the stricture of not destroying. To destroy may be no more than another way of continuing. What has to taken up therefore is another counter to destruction. While it may seem a paradoxical formulation what becomes necessary is a way of giving expression to the presence of a discontinuous continuity. Continuity is at hand because of the refusal of destruction – and it here needs to be noted that what is being refused is the literal destruction of a series of buildings, roads and infrastructure created in the 1980s – while discontinuity is demanded by the imperative of not continuing. The anti-monument would arise as the result of having taken destruction literally. It would be for this reason that the rubble of destruction would have become the exemplary anti-monument. In this context, this would have been an inappropriate response for two reasons. In the first instance, it would have failed to grasp the central role played by vision in the construction of the original urban setting. The original setting allows for the description of its being monumental precisely because of the uniformity of the gaze it demands. While in the second, such a response abandons the strictures and the demands of architecture in the process.

Given that the Boulevard Unirii is a central axis within the city what has to occur is a process of demonumentalization, thought within the confines of a discontinuous continuity, that holds to the necessity of retaining the road. (Reiser and Umemoto refer to this type of possibility as 'an access that is not an axis'.) The same approach has to be case with the buildings alongside the road. Equally the former palace – now the House of Parliament – needs to be repositioned even though it has to retain its current position.

In the case of the Boulevard the plan adopted by Reiser and Umemoto has two interrelated elements. Both are only explicable in terms of demonumentalization. The first involves dropping most of the road beneath the surface. There is an elegant simplicity to this move. Once the road vanishes beneath the surface then its capacity to allow a uniformity of gaze has been transformed. The gaze within a tunnel is devoid of any form of monumentality whatsoever. While eliminating the corridor is essential to the general practice of demonumentalizing the surface remains. Here, in a move that reiterates part of the force of the Kansai Library project and Yokohama, in the place of a flat road the surface would now be a 'mounded park'. The force of the park is twofold. In first place it would attract different types of programmatic possibilities while at the same time it would eschew the possibility of the uniformity of the gaze. There would not be a single view. As such the dominant dictate that controlled the original monumental construction would have been overcome and yet this overcoming would have precluded the necessity of another monument. The counter to the monument – to the process of an urban monumentalism – need not create another monument. For the counter move, and here the counter needs to be envisaged as the instantiation of alterity, to remain architectural, it is almost essential that the construction of another monument be precluded.

The monumental nature of the palace, the second largest existing building (the Pentagon being the largest) comes to be incorporated into the other aspect fundamental to their project namely a major loop system of roads. The importance of the road system is once again explicable in terms of the process of demonumentalization. The loop works to establish connections between parts of the city that were initially separated after the destruction of the 1980s, in order to establish the original monumental structure. The palace would be linked to other buildings that would work to alter the scale of the original building. Its size would be mediated by its coming into connection with previously separated parts of the city, and by the development of infrastructure which would erode the singularity of the original palace by its incorporation within a growing infrastructure. While this aspect of the project would need to be developed in greater detail its importance can nonetheless be situated in relation to the process of demonumentalization.

In sum, therefore, what their submission to the Bucharest 2000 competition involves is a sustained attempt to reconfigure an urban setting utilizing a series of strategies linked to the productive potential within demonumentalization. Again it can be seen that context while not determining the nature of the outcome sets the stage for the orientation of their intervention. The activity is not aimed at the elimination of the fabric's constituent parts. On the contrary, it is driven by the need to link growth to the advent of alterity. Their interplay – the productive presence of growth and alterity – opens up the possibility of an incomplete urbanism. What would make it incomplete is the twofold necessity of demonumentalizing while resisting the incursion of the counter monument. Such a point of departure precludes the possibility that there is a definite form proper to it. There is a continual opening to the extent that the incomplete is held as always in play within finite strategies. Finitude delimited by the work of the incomplete precludes representation, not because of representation's failure, but because their copresence – the copresence of the incomplete and the finite enacted as the plural event – precludes the presence to self and thus the self-completing finality demanded by representation. In not being one there cannot be one thing to represent.

ENDS

These projects can be attributed a specific end. Opening up that end will involve a return to what has already been identified as the staging of architecture. The key to any understanding of architecture's being staged is repetition. And yet, because repetition cannot be attributed either a singular form or an essential nature, repetition has to be more precisely understood as that which accounts for that staging. Since the new in architecture is always conditioned by what has taken place, and thus because any architectural moment will already have been placed, architecture is repetition. Even if the architect forgets the building always remember its being as architecture. The central evaluative and interpretive question therefore concerns the type of repetition that is being staged. What counts as a repetition in architecture cannot be distinguished from the recognition of the ineliminability of function. Function – always already inarticulated with its continually differing formal presence – is that which comes to be repeated in the staging of architecture. This defines the ends of architecture.

These ends are located within a structure of repetition in which there can be both an identification of the presence of that structure and the possibility that within the architecture's own effectuation, within its own activity as architecture, there can be a sustained engagement with that already present determination. In order for an engagement to take place intervention and invention must occur within the prevailing structure of repetition. What has to be opened up is another staging of that which is given to be repeated. For this staging to eschew the incursion of the prescriptive and thus the closure that it brings with it, the present has to have the yet-to-be determined as part of its determination. Inscribing this quality, a quality that is primarily there as an immaterial effect, becomes the activity of the incomplete within architecture. It has the force of a productive negativity working as an opening within the present. And yet, as has already been suggested this opening is not utopian. Rather than yielding a future that is beyond the present, the future is given as an already insistent possibility within and as part of the present. To the extent that this future is sustained, architecture maintains itself as incomplete. The incomplete is given in relation to an engagement with function that is realized by the activity of design. Form does not follow function. Form defines the possibility of alterity within function. This is architecture's other possibility. It is thus its other end.

PART II

ARCHITECTURAL THEORY

INTRODUCTION

The move to architectural theory cannot be thought in terms of an abstraction either from the empirical and historical presence of architecture or from the actual presence of the practice of architecture. Abstraction, in this context, is the necessary refusal of specificity. Once abstraction is removed from a position of centrality the question of the theoretical in architecture returns with greater acuity. The refusal of abstraction has two important consequences. The first is that architectural theory has to be interconnected – perhaps even interarticulated – with the actual activity of architecture. The denial of abstraction means that the theory is not held over to one side as an after event or even as the first part of the move from the pure to the applied. In both instances the theoretical is always one step removed from the architectural.

The second consequence stems from the first. If the theoretical is from the very start concerned with the particularity of the architectural, then how is that relationship to be thought. The argument has to be that it is the thinking of this second consequence, a thinking in which the activity of philosophy and theory combine, that marks out the space for an other formulation of architectural theory. In the following chapters there is a sustained attempt to pursue, in different ways, the two consequences that arise from the impossibility of maintaining the effective presence of theory as abstraction.

Chapters 4 and 5 have interrelated areas of inquiry. Both pursue the problem of thinking the particularity of architecture by deploying the resources from within the history of philosophy to further that end. Readings of Kant and Leibniz in Chapter 4 opens up the ways to take up the complex theme of experience. While it remains the case that a concern with experience – or the impossibility and thus the numbing of experience – is one of the defining motifs of any serious concern with a theory of modernity, the difficulty is attempting to give an explanation of how that concern figures within architectural theory. There cannot be the general question of experience. Again, it has to be specific. How is experience within architecture to be thought? While there are sociological or historical answers to such a question, here the concern is with thinking experience's conditions of possibility. Part of such a project is allowing for a distinction between differing forms of experience. In order to avoid a simple phenomenology what has to be brought into consideration is the connection between experience and the structure of repetition already developed in earlier chapters. It is terms of that interconnection that experience can be seen to involve the important distinction that has already been noted and which has been expressed in terms of the logic of the apart/a part. In this context of this section the defining element concerns the determination of tradition.

The ostensible concern of Chapter 5 is to think through some of the difficulties that are attached to the term 'theory'. Moving between canonical architectural texts and the philosophical and literary critical writings of Blanchot and Bataille, 'theory' becomes a site of constant renegotiation. Drawing on some of the work on Bataille already begun in Chapter 1, the completing and thus totalizing vision assumed to be at work within theory is put to one side in order to allow for a further development of the theme of the incomplete. The central question concerns the nature of the incomplete in architecture. The resource of Blanchot and Bataille are used to develop the question; particular attention is paid to the role of '*désouvrement*' in their work. (This term allows for the presence of the incomplete though, in part, in relation to a productive negativity.) Consequently, rather than assuming there is one complete and final answer to the question of the theoretical it is left to endure as a question. As such its intricacy and the difficulties of its continuing to endure become the site addressed by the chapter.

Chapter 6 takes the question of the theoretical in a different direction. While the demands set by the possibility of alterity and the critical are raised in the earlier Chapters, this chapter is directly concerned with the nature of the experimental in architecture. While never forgetting the constraint imposed by experimentation having to have a site

– a site that can be accounted for in terms of the detailed presentation of the '*in architecture*' in Chapter 1 – in this context what is central is emergence of a site of experimentation taking place in the withdrawal of the interpretive and generative centrality of representation. While there is no attempt to deny that representation is a possible and at times necessary effect of any diagram, experimentation is linked to the emergence of a conception of the diagram that does not take representation as its ground. Allowing representation to be an after effect, works to define experimentation as, in the first place, that which is enacted by the diagram, and in the second, in having to think how the movement from diagrammatic investigation to plan and section and thus to representation is itself going to place. The absence of direct continuity opens up the move from diagram to representation as another site of experimentation.

The concerns of this chapter as is the case for the earlier two are strictly theoretical in so far as they take as their domain of investigation the question: how to think the particularity of the architectural?

4

BUILDING EXPERIENCE

What is the experience of a building? What is the relationship between the building as an event and the event of that experience, its being experienced *as* building? These two questions provide a frame within which building experience can come to be formulated. Building experience – a designation whose stakes remain imprecise – provides access to a possible point of contact, one as much ignored as denied. It can be seen as marking the intersection – between the retention of a phenomenology (as a philosophy of experience) and a type of transcendental idealism (being the philosophical 'approach' most concerned with conditions of possibility). And yet to describe it as an intersection may fail to do justice to the drama and the force of the connection. The intersection could be an abutment or the points of contact may be imbricated. Abutting and imbricating bring with them their own specific formulation of the problem of identity, since, it could be argued, they each involve, in relation to their constitutive elements, an identity giving or sustaining interdependence. The connection, in order that it sustain difference by maintaining relation, needs to be rearticulated by interposing what will be called a differential ontology.[1] The need and the consequences of this addition will emerge in the argument to come. The addition is, however, not a supplement since the task of clarifying the connection and thus of formulating building experience means that in the process of rearticulation they are redefined by it. What is involved here is therefore a type of repetition.

At work, though perhaps as yet underworked, in the attempt to formulate connections and interconnections, an attempt as much philosophical as architectural, is the problem of relation. With relation there emerges the space within, and of, that relation. While these tentative formulations work by joining and relating space and relation it will, nonetheless, be argued in the following that relations are real and even though those relations are not reducible to a straightforward realism, and in different ways can be construed as constitutive of both spacing and the event. Taking these considerations a step further necessitates repeating elements, albeit both briefly and hesitantly, of two important moments within the history of philosophy; one concerned to overcome the possibility of internal relations and the other attempting to extrude relation from its playing a constitutive role in the formulation, perhaps the form, of space. The repetition of these arguments rids them of mere historicality.

The first moment begins with elements of Leibniz's epistolary confrontation with Clarke and thus with Newton. While the second involves taking up some of the consequences that stem from Kant's formulation of space and time in the Transcendental Aesthetic within the *Critique of Pure Reason*. The work of this presentation of space and time is, at least in the first instance, restricted by the text's intentional logic. This restriction provides the possibility of a further opening for the taking up of relation. The importance of relation is linked to the effective nature of its presence. If what is at stake is, for example, the relation between philosophy and architecture then what will be involved is not just the attempt to define the particularity of each but thinking the relation itself. Moreover if space is as Leibniz argues relational then this demands that the relation, rather than being accepted as posited, (its being given and its being as one and the same) should be taken as itself in need of philosophical consideration. If building experience involves the experience of architecture as architecture then such a construal of experience necessitates recourse to the conditions of possibility that allow the 'as' to function. In these possibilities what continually emerges is not simply the presence of relation but the inability to take its determination, and it is usually a determination with the most minimal content, as given.

LEIBNIZ - IMPOSSIBLE RELATIONS

Leibniz's argument with Newton can be seen as having at least two fundamental premises. The first is that substances are not themselves spatial (space is not a predicate of substance). The second is that space involves 'an order of succession' and is therefore relational. The relativity in question is not to be counterposed to an absolute. Since space is the relation between monads any relativity could not pertain to

substance in the singular but to substances in the plural. Monads themselves are not spatial. There is therefore no absolute space in which
substances are located. Within an imaginary Leibnizian philosophical
grammar a possible locative would always be determined by an 'in
relation to . . .'. In other words the spatial location is established, positioned, because of a relation to another substance. Space does not
however exist as an end in itself. Despite the work of intention which
may be taken as demanding such an existence, space is neither self-
referring nor does it admit of self-definition. Indeed Leibniz's presentation of space is defined in terms of time and thus depends upon the
effective presence of a temporal base. This 'dependence' is clear from
the 'Third Letter to Clarke':

> I hold space to be something merely relative, as time is; ... I
> hold it to be an order of coexistences as time is an order of
> successions. For space denotes in terms of possibility, an order
> of things which exist at the same time, considered as existing
> together; (*Elles existent ensemble*) without enquiring into the
> manner of existing. And when things are seen together, one
> perceives that order of things among themselves.[2]

Two aspects of the letter should be noted in advance. The first is the
distinction drawn by Leibniz between things 'existing together' (*elles
existent ensemble*) and their 'manner of existing' (*leurs manières
d'exister*). The second is his use of the term 'ensemble' to describe a
totality without parts and therefore without relations. While both of
these aspects play a pivotal role in any understanding of Leibniz's
position, what is essential in each case is the particular construal that
is given to 'existence'. What is at stake here are the modes of being
proper to that which is presented as spatial relations. A presentation
articulated in temporal terms.

The significant temporal element that arises here is the description
of space as depending upon 'an order of things which exist at the
same time' (*un ordre des choses qui existent en même temps*). This
gives rise to two related questions. First, what is the time of this existence? And second, what of *its* existence? Working with the assumption
of the necessary – and of necessity plural – interarticulation of being
and time, what this second question seeks to elucidate is the mode of
being designated by this time, i.e. the specific ontologico-temporal

concatenation. These questions, which emerge from Leibniz's own formulations, are of singular importance as they gesture – though here it is no more than a gesture – towards the unannounced, and of necessity unannounced, presence of differential ontology. A significant split emerges, a split characterized by relation and distance, in the differing ways in which plurality can be said to be present. The split hinges on the voicing of this presence.

There are two components of this passage that are of immediate interest. The first is the interrelated definitions of space and time. The second is the already mentioned projected twofold distinction within existence. This latter aspect is comprised of what, on the one hand, can be taken to be the assertion of the fact of existence, and on the other of identifying the 'manner' or mode of that existence. While this distinction can always be expressed in terms of the difference between quality and quantity advanced in sections seven and eight of the *Monadology* where Leibniz takes up an important distinction that can be located in Aristotle and which comes to be redeployed by Hegel in the Doctrine of Being in the *Shorter Logic* it will, nonetheless, be essential to find a way of formulating it with greater precision and thus with its having far greater extension.

Space and time are both orders. In the case of space, it is one of 'coexistence'. Again this repeats the exact formulation given by Leibniz in a letter to Des Bosses in 1712, 'Space is an order of coexisting phenomena' [*spatiun fit ordo coexistentium phaeonenorum*].[3] This 'order' exists at 'the same time'. Time sustains space. Consequently it is once again clear that the possibility of space does not simply rely on the presence of monads, but that their existence is temporally defined in terms of a specific present. This establishes why division within the monad has to be precluded. Division, within monads, would mean that not only were they spatial but temporal as well. (It will be vital to note the extent to which, in the end, both these possibilities can be excluded).

The interrelated definition does not just work for space. Time is also defined as an order. Here it is not one that exists between monads at the present; the present time. But rather it involves a relation between monads that exist at different present times; i.e. different points in the 'order of succession'. It is at this stage that two related questions arise. Is this difference purely temporal? Is there not in the very formulation of the distinction between two different presents the involvement of an inherent and absolutely necessary spacing? In other words, even if the distinction is temporal the fact that they are held apart would seem not just to allow for spacing but, more emphatically, would also necessitate the presence of spacing and thus of space. The presence in question would not take the form of an intrusion; on the contrary, it would figure as the *condiditio sine qua non* for temporal succession itself. The challenge that emerges at this point stems from the recognition that if there is this additional spacing, and, that if this spacing is necessary to sustain the identity as well as the formulation of time and space, then it is an addition that falls outside the ambit of the Leibnizian conceptions of both space and time. Pursuing this point involves taking up the posited twofold nature of existence deployed in the description of space in the 'Third Letter to Clarke'.

The distinction drawn by Leibniz between things existing and the manner of existing is, on the surface at least, posed in terms of the difference between the form taken by that which exists and the fact of that existence. These relations will also determine possible existences; possible factual existence. In other words any future existence will not simply involve new spatial relations, as though such relations were no more than a simple addition. The actual role played by these relations is far more significant than that which is suggested by the possibility that they were no more than a mere addition. (The temporality and reality of being an addition needs to be rethought.) Indeed it is the reality of these relations which, while being the articulation of subsequent existences (what Leibniz will have identified as '*les existants*'), will also provide future existences with their conditions of possibility. Leibniz makes this point in the *New Essays on Human Understanding* where he argues that space is:

> ... a relation, an order not only between that which exists (les existants) but furthermore between possible existences *as if they existed*. (les possible *comme s'ils existent*).[4]

Possible existence brings with it a specific problem. While it may seem that all that is at play here is the exemplification of the need to account, on the one hand for the spatiality of possible future existences (the spatiality of relations to come), and on the other of the inclusion of time within space, there is considerably more at stake. Detailing this 'more' is complex.

The first point to note is the use of the expression 'as if', (*comme si*). What this expression indicates is the necessity of relation and yet it is a necessity that exists as a potential. The 'as if' involves a two-fold temporal division. In the first place there is a present necessity. In the second place however there is a potential that, even though it is unactualized, it is nonetheless still present. This gives rise to the question of how the distinction between actual relations (which define space and the present) and futural possible relations (which open up Leibnizian time) is to be understood? Any answer must commence with the recognition that the distinction is not between the present, a specific present, and the future as such. If it were, then the 'as if' would have been rendered otiose. The future is only present in terms of the necessary preconditions for the possibility of the future, namely relation and therefore space; the space of an inherent and implicit spacing. The temporality of the future will involve the 'order of succession' in which time figures as a series of distanced and hence spaced moments. In spite of this figuration, included within any present moment are precisely the preconditions for possible existences at future times. This means therefore that the present is always divided between 'that which exists' (*les existants*) at the present and possible existences whose presence at the present is, in this instance, always mediated by the 'as if'. What is emerging here is a divided present. The division is not sustained by the posited difference – a difference yielding eventual similarity – between universal and particular but pertains to the monad and thus to any of its present moments.

Leibniz makes a related point in section 22 of the *Monadology*. Even though this example does not concern the 'as if', it still occasions the same result, namely that divided present in which the division though initially temporal is, because of the definitional interdependence between space and time, also spatial. Furthermore the co-presence of both space and time, coupled with the nature of that presence, will mean that the division is as much ontological as temporal. Indeed this must be the case if time and being are always already interarticulated rather than simply delimiting each other.[5] ... so every present state of a simple substance is naturally a consequence of the preceding state, in such a way the present is big with the future. (... *le présént y est gros de l'avenir*).[6]

While this may make the present plural, the nature of that plurality is yet to be specified. Positing plurality in this sense raises the question of its relation to Leibniz's celebrated description of the monad as multiplicity in unity. The definition of the monad as multiplicity in unity needs to be understood in connection with elements of Leibniz's presentation of simple substance.

In the *Monadology* simple substance is described as having neither 'extension', nor 'figure' nor 'divisibility'. The monad cannot be affected from outside; it is rather that its capacity for change comes from an 'internal principle'. As the monad changes there must be, Leibniz argues, elements that remain the same. This obviates the possibility of a radical transformation in which the monad would be recreated from within itself as the absolutely new. Change therefore takes place 'by degrees'. It is this description incorporating the co-presence of rest and change that generates one formulation of multiplicity in unity. At section 13 of the *Monadology*, it is expressed in the following *way*: '... it is necessary that in the simple substance there is a plurality of affections and relations (*de rapports*) although there are no parts (*il n'y en ait point de parties*)'.[7]

Even though the consistency of Leibniz's argument in arriving at this conclusion is not in question – since it stems from his definition of a simple substance or monad – what does arise is the problem of how to understand the presence of a relation in which there are 'no parts'. The reason why there is a problem is obvious. It looks as though the two claims are contradictory. How could there be a relation when there are 'no parts'? While it will have to be reworked via greater concentration on the actual specificity of the parts in question, the initial response to the presence of this apparent contradiction must involve indicating that it – the putative contradiction – is based on a misconstrual of the ontological nature of the monad. The monad while being a 'veritable atom' is not subordinated to an ontology of stasis. Taking it as having such an ontology provides the basis of the imputed contradiction. (The ontology of stasis and the logic of identity are themselves interarticulated.) The monad is not a building block. Its mode of being is more complex. It forms a complex. This point is made in his treatment of substance in a letter to De Volder, 23 March/3 April 1699. In arguing against Descartes and the conception of substance as extension he goes on to state that: '... there should be no need to seek any other explanation for the conception of power or force that is the attribute from which change follows and *its subject is substance itself*.'[8]

The 'internal principle' that causes the monad to change is therefore 'force'. (In Latin *vis*). The initial difficulty here is description. Even though the monad is not static, it would also be inappropriate to describe it as *in* a state of becoming. Such a description would mean that there was something *in* that state and as such that 'something' would need its own preliminary ontological description. Force is neither a predicate of substance, nor is it the monad's essence. Expressed accurately, force is that which substance is. What this means is that the mode of being proper to substance is becoming. In other words substance is becoming itself. Here however becoming is not opposed to being. Repeating this position would simply present, perhaps re-present becoming within the opposition of logical exclusion that informs and which comes to be articulated as the Platonic heritage. The way in which this logic unfolds, and thus the heritage comes to be repeated – though repeated within similitude – is that either one term excludes the other or that becoming is understood as a species of being and therefore subordinate to it. What is at stake is, on the contrary, the possibility of the co-presence of being and becoming. In other words one significant conclusion to be drawn from this redescription is that the assertion that a specific monad has a particular designation – its being a given *x*, or in Leibniz's terms, its having a given 'perception' *x* – does not occlude 'force' and therefore does not preclude its having an ontology of becoming. Force is present but not actualized within and as a particular. Rather than being actually present it is primordially present.[9] It is thus that the monad is comprised of two forms of presence which are co-present in their difference. The monad therefore becomes the site of anoriginal plurality marked by the presence of an irreducibility that is ontological in nature. Its being this site may work against the text's intentional logic, none the less its presence as a site of irreducibility is compatible with the presentation of the monad's own logic. In other words the monad becomes the site of an ontological complex in which complexity is anoriginal and involves ontological irreducibility.

This description is reinforced by Leibniz's construal of perception and the nature of the ontological difference between perception and appetition. As the difference is ontological and therefore differential rather than one where difference signals no more than the presence of mere diversity or descriptive variety, what is emerging is the need for a further elaboration of the monad as an anoriginally plural event.[10] The presence of anoriginal ontological difference entails the primacy of difference (difference as differential) over the Same. The differential yields a conception of difference that is comprised of incompatible values. Identity, in this instance, becomes the belonging together of the ontologically different. (As an aside, it worth pointing out that the co-presence of actual and potential being (understood here as stasis and becoming) undermines, from within, the Platonic critique of Heraclitus as developed in both the *Theaetetus* and the *Cratylus*. Furthermore it does not necessitate the hierarchy of 'being' generated by Aristotle in both the *Categories* and the *Physics*).

Perception, as is clear from *Monadology* section 15, is a representation. In other words it is the state of the monad at a given point in chronological time. It is what it is and thus it is how it presents itself at a given present. However what it is at the present, its self-presentation, is not and moreover can never be coextensive with the monad itself, because the 'itself' is anoriginally plural. In addition, though relatedly, this point can be argued for on the basis of the law of the identity of indiscernibles as well as in connection to the ontology proper to appetition. The monad is the co-presence of perception and appetition. It is the co-presence therefore of the ontology of stasis, its being what it is, its perception, and a potential which is present but which demands an explication in terms of the ontology of becoming. The result of this situation is that the monad contains, indeed is comprised of, two different ontological realms. Their continual, though nonexcluding, interaction is the work of the monad and to that extent the mode of being proper to the monad is a continual becoming, similar to the Heraclitean ῥέον ἀεί (always flowing).

This is a becoming whose precise stakes remain to be formulated. Now, while this co-presence is not what Leibniz means by 'multiplicity in unity' it indicates that the unity is in fact comprised of a plurality or multiplicity at a far more profound level. In section 16 of the *Monadology*, Leibniz formulates multiplicity in unity thus: 'We have in our selves experiences of a multiplicity in simple substances when we find that the least thought of which we are conscious involves variety in its object.[11] Multiplicity here is closer to the plurality to which he refers in the letter to De Volder. It occurs only on the level of quality and enables one monad to be distinguished from another. What has been identified above as an ontological plurality is a state of affairs not recognized as such by Leibniz but to which his position is committed. The question that must be answered is, whether or not this plurality involves relations without parts. Prior to answering this question however, it is essential to note Kant's formal attempt to exclude relation by extruding it from his consideration of space by repositioning it (relation) within the domain of cognition.

KANT - EXTRUDING RELATION

It is in terms of this repositioning that Kant can be interpreted as trying to differentiate his philosophical stance from the one held by Leibniz. With Kant, rather than space emerging as that which is, of necessity, articulated temporally, (and where time is premised upon an ineliminible though unannounced spacing) it becomes the precondition for the possibility of 'outer intuition'. It is, in other words, the necessary precondition for the possibility of the representation of appearance and thus of experience. This point, plus an opening distancing of relation is expressed by Kant at B42:

> Space does not represent any property of things in themselves, nor does it represent them in their relation to one another. That is to say that space does not represent any determination that attaches to the objects themselves, and which remains even when abstraction has been made of all the subjective conditions of intuition. For no determination, whether absolute or relative, can be intuited prior to the existence of things to which they belong, and none, therefore, can be intuited *a priori*.[12]

Without attempting to trace the totality of Kant's argument in the *Transcendental Aesthetic*, some background is needed to prepare for an examination of the position announced in this passage.

Within Kant's critical philosophy – his precritical writings on space are still explicitly influenced by Leibniz – it is vital to clarify what is meant by appearance and object. At B34 their independent existence is checked by their being defined in terms of each other. This takes place in the following way: 'The undetermined object of an empirical intuition is entitled appearance' (*Der unbestimmte Gegenstand einer empirischen Anschauung heisst Erscheinung*).

The use of the qualifying term *unbestimmte* (undetermined) should be noted since what is at play here is the initial formulation of a distinction between the 'matter' and the 'form' of the appearance. In terms of 'matter' the appearance is 'undetermined' and to that extent appearances cannot be formally distinguished from each other. The object, *der Gegenstand*, is pure objectivity. On the other hand determination and relation derive their conditions of existence from form. Form makes them possible. It is thus that the distinction between matter and form is at the same time a distinction between the *a posteriori* and the *a priori*. Form does not pertain to sensation itself. It is, to use Kant's formulation, 'found in the mind *a priori*'. Space is the 'form of all appearances . . .'

In the passage under consideration, space cannot represent either a property or a relation because they are both determinations. The latter, the *Bestimmungen*, are only explicable in terms of the concepts and categories of the understanding. While it is tempting to view the distinction between that which is *Unbestimmte* and the subsequent *Bestimmung* as temporal in nature – the 'subsequent' marking a purely temporal difference – this would be to miss the force of Kant's transcendental logic. What is in fact being laid out is an architectonic not a series of temporal measures. Moreover, identifying the difference in this way runs the risk of psychologizing Kant. Nonetheless it is precisely because what is at stake here is a architectonic, that a difficulty emerges. It occurs in the following line from the passage cited above (B42).

> For no determinations (*Bestimmungen*) whether absolute or relative, can be intuited prior to the existence of things (*vor dem Dasein der Dinge*) to which they belong and none therefore can be intuited a priori. (My emphasis).

The way in which this formulation concludes is its least problematic component. The difficulty hinges on the use of the expression 'prior to' (*vor dem*). If it cannot be given temporal priority, where the move, would have been understood as taking place from one moment to the next, then the question must arise as to the nature of this 'prior to' Kant's overall argument is clear. There can be no intuition, a determination 'prior to' the intuition of the existence of those things to which such determinations properly belong. It follows therefore that none can be intuited *a priori*. As a beginning it is important to note that the 'prior to' marks and sustains the point at which the difference between the *a posterior* and the *a priori* occurs. The 'prior to' therefore introduces a space.

How is this space and hence the presence of a specific relation to be understood? (The relation in question is not the one either joined to or envisaged by this spacing but the one it enjoins, since space here works in terms of the co-presence of distancing and relating; so the 'prior to' works to distance as well as to relate.) The problem bears upon representation. The 'prior to' is introduced within a general argument concerning representation. The problem concerns the representability of this initial and founding relation of distance. What is at play here is, that despite difference – present in the instance as the implicit relation of distance as well as the explicit distinction between the *a posteriori* and the *a priori* – engendering the possibility for the intuition of determinations, it is also the case that such differences cannot themselves be objects of intuition since difference provides the basis for intuition itself. The 'prior to' involved a relation – a relation of distance – that, despite being constitutive of the event in which sensibility, intuition and the concepts of the understanding come to be deployed as consecutive elements within the architectonic (see A19), cannot and hence does not figure as itself – that is as an inaugurating relation – within the event. The relation is 'outside' representation. Even though the 'prior to' is not be thought of as temporal, if temporality is given either a progressive or serial sense, it still cannot be denied that the present event is comprised of internal relations – relations involving subsequent determinations – but where that which is subsequent is itself dependent upon an initial spacing marked by the 'prior to'. It is the spacing that cannot be reduced to a 'pure intuition'. Indeed this last point has to be the case since the 'prior to', as has already be indicated, marks, while sustaining, the point of difference between the *a posteriori* and the *a priori*. It is itself neither one nor the other, in this context the 'prior to', as relation, provides both of them with the conditions of possibility. What cannot be represented is spacing as constitutive of the plural event.

The restriction of representation has a number of different sources. It is the obvious consequence of Kant's general argument that space is not relational but a 'pure intuition'. Furthermore it is, *pace* the text's intentional logic, the result of space being the inaugural place of difference, as was identified above. Finally, and in more gene terms, it also involves the actual construal of the unidimensional nature of space itself. This is formulated at B39 in the following terms '. . . we can represent to ourselves only one space; and if we speak of diverse spaces, we mean thereby only parts of the one and the same unique space'.

It should be noted that Kant argues the same point in relation to time at B47. 'Time has only one dimension; different times are not simultaneous but successive'. Once again what is excluded is an event whose plurality is temporal. Part of the general argument here is that the presentation of space and time is such that neither could lend itself to what could best be termed a doubling, within which there is either, on the one hand, a co-presence or, on the other, a repetition that would work to render an event as internally, and therefore constitutively, plural. Space and time can never be reincorporated back into the event, although the exclusion does not refer to that which could never have been included. On the contrary it refers to relations that found subsequent divisions within the architectonic. It is this relation which puts into question the very systematicity of the architectonic. In specific terms therefore it has begun to founder at the moment of its founding because of the necessary presence of an inaugurating difference. It is at this precise point, namely with the formulation of the unidimensional nature of time and space within the *Critique of Pure Reason*, that there is an important analogy with Leibniz. While recognizing the problems of any analogy, it is still one worth pursuing.

In a letter to Arnauld (30 April 1687), and as part of a larger argument that there cannot be a multitude 'without true unities' (*sans des veritable unités*) he goes on to argue that: 'It has always been believed that one and being are reciprocal things. One thing is being, the other thing is beings; but the plural supposes the singular and (*le pluriel suppose le singulier*) where there is not one being there will not be several beings'.[13]

What is significant here is the description of multiplicity as involving singularity such that the multiple is a complex made up of particulars. While this is a position that is, if only in part, belied by his own description of multiplicity in unity as advanced in the *Monadology*, it characterizes a general presentation of the multiple within a philosophical thinking that incorporates positions as apparently diverse as those of Descartes and Heidegger. In each case what is always excluded is a singular that is plural. Division, even plurality, will always demand external relations. The tradition, working with the assumption of an initial singularity, posits a movement into relation.[14] The result being that no division can ever be projected as taking place except as between two given unities. The division is also positioned as both ontologically and temporally consequent to that of the constitutive unities since they must, of necessity, be posited as already existing. The division, or the plurality, can never be within, either the unity, or the singularity or the 'veritable atom'. The irony is that it is precisely this state of affairs, i.e. a plural singular anoriginally present that is at work, in different though foundational ways, in the work of both Leibniz and Kant. It is thus that it is essential to recognize that the anoriginal presence of a plural singular provides ways of rethinking elements of a transcendental idealism. This thereby facilitates the incorporation of the transcendental – perhaps a repeated and thus redeemed transcendental – into ontological philosophy.

It is in terms of the plural singular that it is possible to return to the question posed above as to whether ontological plurality involved relations without parts. It should be added that inherent in this question lies the problem of the possibility of thinking relation independently of spacing. This is the central architectural question because the very fact of its impossibility raises again the difficulty of formulating the interplay, and hence relation, of spacing and experience; building experience of and within the building. The twofold marking building experience needs to be retained.

BUILDING - PLURAL RELATIONS

Ontological plurality cannot be straightforwardly identified with multiplicity in unity. And yet, however, there is a sense in which the possibility of such a multiplicity is dependent upon ontological plurality. This emerges with greatest clarity, as has already been suggested, in the distinction established by Leibniz in the *Monadology* between perception and appetition. What is important about this distinction is not the detail – that is, it is not the different ways in which the monad can present itself – but rather the nature of the co-presence of perception which presents itself as a representation and appetition. It is, of course, not a simple co-presence insofar as the possibility of a future perception – the monad presenting itself as a specific further x – is dependent upon appetition. Appetition is defined in the *Monadology* section 15 in the following way:

The activity of the internal principle which produces change or passage from one perception to another may be called appetition. It is true that the appetite (*l'appétit*) cannot always fully attain to the whole perception at which it aims, but it always obtains some of it and attains to new perceptions.[15]

The significant point is that this co-presence establishes what could quite appropriately be termed an *ensemble*. The ontologically plural event is a type of ensemble. It has 'parts'(*des parties*). However the term *ensemble* already has currency. It should not be forgotten that Leibniz has previously used it (*ensemble*) in the 'Third Letter to Clarke' to describe the existence of an 'order of things which exist at the same time'. They exist together and as such establish relations that comprise space. Space can be said to exist in its being articulated in terms of a temporally defined simultaneity of presence. While *ensemble* – the original ensemble – is a term providing an apposite description of the presence of a relation between existent monads at a given and contemporaneous point in time, it is not, at this stage, descriptive of the monad itself. The ensemble thus far is a collection of particulars, a plurality of constitutive parts, an ensemble. (In the same way Kant's' 'diverse spaces' are only parts of the 'same unique space' [B39]. His conception of allness' (*Allheit*) or 'totality' (*Totalität*) has the same structure in that it is presented as 'plurality considered as unity' [B111]).

The sense in which the monad is an ensemble is of course quite different. (As a methodological point it is worth noting that the term's repetition frees it from, while linking it to, its already existent uses.) Here the ensemble in question involves the belonging together of that which resists synthetic unity. The existence of the monad as an already existent ensemble, means that the monad is an anoriginal ensemble; i.e. an ensemble in which differential plurality is not a consequence of the event, on the contrary it is constitutive of the event – the relational ensemble – itself. It follows from this that part of what would be involved in giving greater precision to the mode of being proper to the monad would be to explicate becoming in terms of anoriginal plurality. This is an explication sanctioned, if not demanded, by Leibniz's own formulations.

There are two reasons for maintaining the distinction between a perception and appetition and not allowing their difference to blur.

The first is that in order for the monad to have a given perception x there must already have been a fundamental difference between perception and appetition. The identity of the perception is sustained by the presence of difference. It provides parts of the perception's conditions of possibility and therefore difference becomes a transcendental precondition for identity. The second reason is related to the first in that it underlines the monad's diremptive existence; remembering that the diremption is internal to the monad and not an external relation. Here the division refers to the possibility, already inscribed in the monad, of its having different perceptions. The consequence of this already present inscription is that it means that the perception *itself* can never be co-extensive with the monad *itself*. (Even if in both cases the nature of the 'itself' remains to be clarified, it should, nonetheless, be stated in advance that their difference involves both ontology and presence.) Describing this coextensivity involves, as has already been indicated, an ontological difference. Difference marked by the co-presence of the different. The monad, as an ensemble, is ontologically plural. The possibility of thinking the monad, a possibility excluded by elements of Leibniz's own work and yet also demanded by them – the same point will, in addition, be true for Kant is the possibility of thinking plurality at the present. What this envisages is a plural present, where the plural is no longer simple complexity, ornamentation or the multiplicity of particulars but is ontological and temporal in nature. Thinking architecture involves precisely the actualization of this possibility. The plural is not an evaluative term, it is only to be opposed to the singular on the levels of intention and interpretation. While there will be a link between plurality and the avant-garde, thus saving the avant-garde from the charge of being no more than a recusant, plurality must also be implicated in that which is intended to be monological. In the end function will yield to plurality by yielding up its capacity to provide architecture with its telos.

It is here that thinking impinges upon experience since it can be argued that what is experienced is exactly this plurality, in that central to, as well as constitutive of experience will be a multiplicity of relations. And yet when the experience is forced to find expression the conceptual apparatus within which this is constrained to take place and thus to be expressed is found wanting. Here the limit involves misrecognition as forgetting. Now, having come this far, it remains the case that the general argument concerning experience, plurality and the problem of expression – experience's expression – as outlined above, still lacks precision for it leaves open the question of what it is that has been found wanting? As an opening move in formulating a response to this question, it is essential to begin with thinking or to be more exact with the preliminary question, with what is thinking undertaken? After all, what thinks architecture? Architectural thinking is best considered in terms of its being thinking.

Within the Kantian heritage the answer to the question of thinking is straightforward. It is the understanding. This position is expressed by Kant in the *Logic* thus '. . . the understanding is the faculty of thinking, that is, of bringing the presentations of the senses under rules. . . . We cannot think or use our understanding otherwise than according to certain rules.[16]

After having made this point Kant goes on to restate the position advanced in the *Critique of Pure Reason* concerning the universality of the rules of the understanding. He then adds that:

Insight into these rules can therefore be gained a priori independently of any experience, because they contain, without discrimination between objects, merely the conditions of the use of the understanding itself, be it pure or empirical.[17]

Within the *Critique of Pure Reason* it is not until the 'Table of Categories' that relation emerges as one of the 'original pure concepts of synthesis that the understanding contains within itself a priori' (B106). Relation here (*Relation*) is not, terminologically, the relation posited earlier. At B42 the relation (*Verhältniss*) in question involves a relationship in which a determination takes place. Relation within the table of categories involves an abstract formulation of possible relations with subsequent determinations, e.g. causality. The point of connection between '*Verhältniss*' and '*Relation*' is that they both depend upon, while also resisting, the incorporation of the interplay of distancing and relating, i.e. spacing. It is, of course, the spacing that is constitutive of an inaugural and founding difference (e.g. between the *a priori* and the *a posteriori*) that sustains the basis of the distinctions between sensibility, intuition and the understanding. Consequently in the case of the understanding, what cannot be known *a priori* is that which differentiates the *a priori* from the *a posteriori*. This elusive presentation eludes because it is implicated in a plurality that is not a totality of particulars. Plurality here founds are putative original identity by founding identity as one of the after effects of inaugural difference.

The difference takes place within ontology because incorporated within the event is a division, a spacing, that resists synthesis. The event is therefore reworked and an initial diremption recovered. As such, of course it becomes the site of doubling or of repetition. The problem this poses is that what has to be represented is a plural space and yet it is exactly this state of affairs that cannot be 'thought' and thus represented by the understanding, thereby opening up the larger problem of the representation of plurality. Grasping the problem demands the recognition that the limit in question is not cognitive. It is historical. Within philosophy, history has to be rethought as the continual interdetermination of repetition and tradition. (Here continuity has the same form as Heraclitean 'strife'; as such it precludes the possibility of essentializing and unifying the process of inter-determination.)[18] the Kantian conception of the understanding needs to be reworked in terms of tradition where tradition is understood as the determination in advance. The determination becomes the rule. This attempt to rework the understanding will yield an approach to building experience.

AN ARCHITECTURAL RELATION

These considerations provide an approach to architecture insofar as architectural thinking as thinking will have to incorporate inaugural difference and the complex it engenders. This allusion to a complex may seem to suggest that the incorporation is unnecessary as the concepts of function, ornament, etc would on their own be adequate to deal with the building as a complex. However this would only be true if the complex in question were a totality of particulars. The complexity of building experience does not take such a totality as its actual object. And yet the work of tradition operates with such a conception of complexity. The consequence of this limitation is then the object and act of experience are devalued in the particular process in which the determination and hence the constraint are given priority. The complex needs to be redeemed by overcoming the twofold reduction of plurality to either its being the addition to unity or no more than *disjecta membra*. In turn this will allow for a rethinking of the constraint. Breaking the automatic link between experience and cognition by the incorporation of tradition does not simply introduce and at the same time open up general political considerations, it also introduces a politics of experience. It is this which is deployed in any explanation of the way in which experience can come to be impoverished.

If tradition involves a type of repetition in which what is repeated is conditioned and determined by the reign of the Same, then this continuity enacts a repetition on at least two levels. Enactment in the restricted sense introduces plurality. However the plurality in question is linked to the operation of power which in turn turns on a type of forgetting. The consequence of this interplay is that the response to repetition within the Same cannot be the interpretive and constructive strategy of deregulation. (The constraint of constraint remains.) This would do no more than counter repetition with an active forgetting. It also overlooks the intrusion of the political into repetition, especially repetition governed by the Same.

The way buildings that seek and enact continuity – i.e. those whose site is within the repetition of the Same – are plural is that in the midst of that act, what comes to be reworked is the inscription of continuity and thus of a specific politics within the building. The politics of building – e.g. the politics of domesticity are co-present with function though not reducible to it. The inscription which it must be added will be an ineliminable component of every building, works by doubling. The event doubled through repetition releases inaugural difference. The building becomes a plural site of which the traditional function is but a single trope because of the recognition that contemporaneous with this, as the building's logic, is the politics of that building. The possible dominance of either logic or politics will depend upon the relative effect of forgetting, remembering and experience.

The risk of plurality means that the determination in advance – the work of tradition – tries to orchestrate a state of affairs in which function becomes the object of experience and that where an addition is deemed to be no more than ornamentation – architectural excess – and therefore is not considered to be an intrinsic part of the building. Experience presented as always open becomes limited in being delimited. It is inextricably marked by the necessity of a forgetting that brings about a foreclosure of the possibility of the experience of plurality. The capacity to experience plurality within the continuity enacted by the determination in advance amounts to a repetition that breaks with a repetition of the Same by opening a space. It is this that gives rise to the possibility of an experience in which the building is given again and anew within that space. The logic of the again and the new becomes constitutive of that internal relation, a plurality that opens – a relation of difference – which sanctions judgement. Judgement is not premised on the forgetting of forgetting, but on the recognition of forgetting as forgetting.

There needs to be a distinction drawn therefore between buildings which, in coming to be repeated, are thereby experienced in terms of plurality and those which, because of the heterological relationship between the concepts and categories that determine the possibility of interpretation engender a pause, an interpretive spacing in which the preconditions for the possibility of experience, namely the spacing, fails to be filled immediately. This particular form of opening marks a hiatus in the determining effect of tradition. It is in relation to this hiatus that it is possible to rethink the concept of the avant-garde. Furthermore it is in terms of this pause that it is possible to give a location to the experience of anoriginal plurality in that what comes to be experienced is precisely that which, because of its inability to be synthesized in terms of the dominant categories and concepts of interpretation – this is the work of tradition – opens a space. It is no longer the case that there is both housing and something in addition. There will always be the presence of that which houses; however housing *per se* no longer provides the object of interpretation with its telos. The telos only endures in the absence of it being, or having, a determining effect. Spacing introduces the need for judgement. The need arises not at the moment of undecideability but at the site of irreducibility.

In relation to the buildings of continuity, repetition breaks the reduction of building to housing. Arising out of this break are the transcendental conditions for judgement. In both cases judgement is only possible when it is linked to the plural. The former demands that experience has overcome forgetting because there can be no judgement within the repetition of the Same – the house fulfilling its function since there is no site of evaluation. Opening the site will always involve repetition and doubling. In the case of the pause as experience – the initial opening within experience – judgement is inextricably linked, in terms of its preconditions, to the maintenance of that spacing. (This amounts to a repositioning of the transcendental.) In sum therefore the stakes of building experience only come to the fore in the inevitable move to judgement; in other words in the opening and the spacing of plurality.[19]

5

BUILDING PHILOSOPHY

TOWARDS ARCHITECTURAL THEORY

Starting with a city, with a writing that situates itself in relation to a city, is to begin with a complex set up. The story – the interconnection between writing and the city – is itself already complicated. As a site, this particular moment of writing turns around a place that, in resisting its own self-absorption, opens up the possibility that it may be the place *par excellence*. Maurice Blanchot writing in 1964 about Berlin, describes it, almost inevitably, as yielding 'the problem of division'.[1] And yet, with Berlin the divisions came to be posed on three different levels; the political, the economic and the metaphysical. Prior to taking up the question of the division – taking it up and allowing its own complication to generate that thinking of division that engenders complexity because it is sustained by it – it is essential to turn to another short, indeed emphatically short text by Blanchot. In a letter addressed to Claire Nouvet and published under the title *Enigma*, Blanchot offers a brief commentary on Mallarmé; specifically on his reworking of Edgar Allen Poe's original formulation of the relationship between architecture and literature.[2] Despite its own internal convolutions this brief excursion will not just allow a return to *Berlin* – now the name of Blanchot's earlier text – but a return, a better return, a return now informed, to two other places, in which the relation architecture/philosophy seems to have been posed. Rather than delimiting their detail at this stage, in this instance these places can be provisionally identified as the body and the urban.

Already these terms bring with them the problem of metaphors and thus language. After all does the body in question involve a literal presence or mere phrasing? It is worth noting that the body – in being a site of calculation as well as order – was never just a metaphor. This point comes to be repeated throughout architectural treatises. Not only is the point made clearly by Vitruvius in *De architectura*, it inheres in his mode of expression. Rather than the work of metaphors the body and the building have an analogical relation.

As in the human body, (*Uti in hominis corpore*) from cubit, foot, palm, inch, and other small parts comes the symmetric quality of eurhythmy; so it is in the completed building. (*sic est in operum perfectionibus.*)

(1, c, II: 4)[3]

Not only will the problem of the body endure, the question of its involving no more than just language, metaphors and thus the retention of a specific vocabulary will become more demanding. What would need to be pursed is how this analogy works. Hence what would return would be the question of the body. Taken as an end itself the body will never have been enough. It will always have been more than itself. They same opening considerations can be brought to bear upon the 'urban'.[4]

Returning to the letter in question, within it Blanchot's task was to examine the possible priority attributed to the ethical within the any thinking of literature. Mallarmé is used first of all to offer the possibility of 'a magical architecture' which whilst having rules, these rules remain unknown. In Mallarmé's terms '... they make themselves mysterious on purpose.' Added to this already difficult possibility is the further claim that what holds the Mallarméan endeavour in place is a deviation from the evocation of rule and mystery and the positing of an anteriority that is both prior and productive. And yet, the presence of the rule biding its time within an anteriority, rather than an external constraint, marks the presence, for Blanchot, not just of the interpretive difficulty of the work, Mallarmé's problematic presence, but of his singularity as poet. Blanchot is acutely aware of this problematic terrain. Indeed Blanchot's scrupulous readings of Mallarmé have always been attentive to this issue. Within those readings this anteriority emerges as 'the unworking of being' (*le désouvrement de l'etre*. 138/110) A productive anteriority that is measured by its '*désouvrement*' – and the force of this term must be understood as a productive negativity resisting the logic of negation – is already a questioning not of the *arché* itself but of the nature of any *arché* that is thought to inhere within architectural practice, though equally within the activity of philosophy.[5] The question that arises does not concern having to establish the link between Blanchot, Mallarmé and architecture, that would be a mere matter of application, rather it touches on the possibility, perhaps the necessity, of thinking architecture once it has become possible to recast the productive presence of these points of inception. Guiding this thinking is the demanding reality that, once essentialism in all its forms is held in abeyance and with the result that the view of theory has become plural, and because its gaze now falls on an unsettled site unsettling the gaze itself, philosophy and architecture will be shown to have been marked by an insistent irreducibility. It insists even though the repetition of tradition's own dominance has sought to preclude the productive inscription of that insistence.

Rather than a form of prevarication, beginning in this way opens up what is fundamental to the nature of theory. Theory is after all the delimitation both of a gaze and of an object. At stake here, both in Blanchot and elsewhere because of its inherently extensive nature, is a play of limits. Neither the unlimited in itself, nor the limit as such, nor moreover a happy correspondence, though in the end it will always have been unhappy, in which one worked to delimit the other. What is both difficult and yet fundamental at this point is the nature of the relationship between production and presence. Of this complex set-up, as it is formulated by Mallarmé, Blanchot offers the following comment – at its heart lies the question of an architectural theory.

> One will understand, I hope, that if I speak of contradictions, it is better to experience their necessity. The pure surging from the source. And nevertheless the calculations which only act by slipping away. Or the intellectual armature that composes itself (space, blank, silence), thus work and mastery. And nevertheless to contain what lightning of instinct, simply life, virgin, in its synthesis, and illuminating everything. Innate and setting rules for itself; anterior and simply life, virgin. Contradictions without conciliation; it is not a question of dialectics.[6]

Perhaps the opening question here should concern the nature of the relationship between 'work and mastery'? While this is the central question evoking as it does the intrusion of philosophy's own conception of the architect – a conception that stems from the conflation of God and architect in Hegel to the description of the builder in Aristotle as always governed and regulated by the *arché* – it needs the setting provided by the difficult possibility of 'contradictions without conciliation'.

In general, contradictions become the identification of what within the tradition of philosophical thinking yields an intolerable state of affairs. Whether it is taken on the level of logic, or as present in the life world, contradiction will demand a form of resolution. Resolution is conciliation; it is finitude without the infinite. Here, of course, contradiction and paradox bring with them the very problems that they seek to identify. And yet contradiction taken at its most elementary is neither tolerable nor intolerable in itself. It is rather that contradictions demand resolution – an enforcing conciliation – once they are viewed as structured either by the logic of identity or by the work of dialectics. Conciliation – its needs and its possibility – arise therefore from this conception of work, or this particular logic. Resolution is an effect. Consequently to write of 'contradictions without conciliation' is not to posit an irresolvable set-up given by the logic of identity or dialectics, but to allow for their abeyance and thus the opening up of a situation in which contradiction and thus conciliation demand other forms of thinking. This is precisely what Blanchot means when he states that of the envisaged situation, 'it is not a question of dialectics'. The demanding problem here is of course – of what is it a question?

In responding to this demand it is possible to effect a specific translation that involves a necessary return to the architectural. This occurs once the body is allowed to play an exemplary role within architectural thinking – it is a role that is as much present within Vitruvius and Alberti as it is within more contemporary formulations of bodily presence (cf. Alberti, *De re aedificatoria*, Book 9, 7). The move from this initial set up to the contemporary is not a move from the unified body to the affirmation of *disjecta membra*. The latter would be the literally fragmented and disrupted body; the architectural correlate would have to run through these differing possibilities. Rather, in the place of exactitude – understood here as conciliation or as resolution – there needs to be a different understanding of unity and thus of an architectural, thus bodily, belonging together. Disruption and the fragmentary are only there in terms of another belonging together. The way this would have to be pursued is in terms of a project of having to think the relationship between the architectural and what Blanchot has described as the 'exigency of the fragmentary'. With such a formulation the fragment would no longer be opposed to unity. Once their specificity – the individual determinations of unity and the fragmentary – have to be thought outside of the structure of contradiction, then thinking the relationship between architecture and the fragmentary becomes a project which, of necessity, demands an inaugural repetition and thus a renewal of thinking. Pursuing this point entails recognizing that rather than the tradition of moving between the unitary and the fragmentary what would have become productive was their already imbricated presence. One would have already been part of the other. It will be vital to return to this problematic formalism since what it suggests is a formal possibility where finitude, what can equated with the demand for form, is copresent with that which would resist complete instantiation. The latter would be the fragmentary in the guise of the incomplete.

Staying with the body, it may be that the possibility of this site – a site other than that of completion – has already been gestured at by Bataille. In sum it is a question that resolves around the 'sick tooth'. What is the architecture? – though equally what is the philosophy? – after the sick tooth?

> Beyond all knowledge there is non-knowledge and the one who would be absorbed in the thought that beyond his knowledge he knows nothing – even were he to have within him Hegel's inexorable lucidity – would no longer be Hegel, but a painful tooth in Hegel's mouth. Would a sick tooth alone be missing from the great philosopher?[7]

Here, it is a question of housing the 'sick tooth'; or, perhaps, beginning with the possible reality of its already having been housed. What then of this tooth? A way of reading Bataille's question is to give it greater range. It is not absolutely central that it be restricted to Hegel. His 'mouth' however must be the initial point of departure since what is raised is the presence of lack. In regards to Hegel the question of the tooth turns on the possibility that what was lacking from the project of 'absolute knowledge' was the inscription of lack. Within

Bataille there is the recognition of the impossibility of the project of complete knowledge, absolute knowledge and thus the finality of epistemological exhaustion. Arguing for that recognition – arguing that is for the affirmed centrality of the incomplete – has become the province of philosophy once philosophy is no longer envisaged as the work of system. Most recently the actual structure of argument has been advanced by deconstruction in the precise sense that fundamental to the strategy of deconstruction has been the attempt to trace the foundering of the project of logocentrism. It has to be the case however that there are other possibilities for an asystemic mode of philosophical thinking which can be articulated in areas that, while adjacent to it, are not formulated within the philosophical space opened by deconstruction. Here, of course, it is quite clearly a question of the nature of the plurality that works within building philosophy. In other words, it is not plurality itself that is of central concern but the way plurality works by holding a metaphysics of the essence to one side. At work are other openings. The central issue here is not a critique of the essential *per se*, but an attempt to pluralize the essence and in so doing to allow the sites architecture/philosophy to have opened up. They will become the differing topoi – containing different topoi – in which the play of conflicting identity will be acted out. The continuity of its being acted out – the acting out of the continuity of identity-in-conflict – in the end comprises the identities of both philosophy and architecture. As such it sets the scene in which the question of their relation needs to be posed.

These openings ought not to be given the force of having provided any new foundations. To the extent that '*désoeuvrement*' – a productive negativity resisting its own negation – plays a productive role, then allocating it the role of a foundation would not only hypostasize the negative, it would also fail to recognize that what is involved cannot be thought in terms of an excluding either/or; i.e. either there is unity or there is the disruption of the all occurring because of a sustained fragmentation of the given. Indeed the contrary is the case since what emerges is the difficult possibility that production always needs to be accounted for in terms of the inscription of that which eschews mastery. Whether it be given in terms of the consequences of thinking Bataille's conception of poetry or the role of negativity in Blanchot, what has to be pursued is the way this generates a conception of production and as well as praxis that resists the hold of a founding *arché* precisely because the tradition of the *arché* brings with it a notion of priority – incorporating evaluation and time – that is no longer appropriate to any account of production. It should not be thought however that the force of this position can only be attributed to the names Bataille and Blanchot. Since, it is not only the case that architecture could come to be informed by other complex conceptions of presence and transformation necessitating a similar type of thinking, it is also true that what is of central importance here is the thinking in question. There are, however, counter positions; other responses to the 'tooth'. It is worth noting elements of these other possibilities since they bring with them two interrelated sites of activity. At this stage their importance lies in the orientation they give to what has emerged as the incomplete.

The first counter concerns the response to the impossibility of eliminating an inscribed unmasterability. While the second becomes the promulgation of that conception of invention which attempts to counter the impossibility of mastery with a formulation of developments that fail to take the question of time – including built time and historical time – into consideration. The first position, and it is there within Bataille's writings tormenting his actual formulations, concerns the possibility of either lament or melancholia. Rather than a recognition of the productive potential of the negative, loss becomes linked to a lament for mastery, or a more generalized melancholia in which thinking becomes pervaded by the work of an unspecified loss. From this position philosophy and architecture become enmeshed within the emergent need to dwell aporetically. It is vital here that the aporetic is not read as an emotional let alone a moral state. In the same way countering lament with affirmation should not be interpreted as counterposing melancholia and joy. Affirmation is more demanding; fundamentally it is the asserted presence of another and thus different form of realism.

An important connection exists between the attempt to counter loss – a move normalizing thus naturalizing loss – and the failure to allow the question of time to be taken as having a determining effect both on the presentation of philosophy and the formulation of programme within architecture. Leaving to one side, at this stage, the reality of built time – the time at work and effective within the building's structuration – the time in question is twofold. In the first place it is the one in which the constraints of theory are given. From one perspective the work of theory orientates itself around a given object that is reproduced through time such that the continuity of an informed vision maintains the work of theory because of the continuity of the object and thus the inherent continuity of the time through which it can be taken to unfold. Theory, both in an etymological sense, and in the more contemporary version, refers to a vision that contemplates, views, accompanies or runs along side its object. What is precluded is the possibility that the division between vision and object, for example, once subject to analysis or investigation would cease to be theoretical since there would no longer be the founding division on which the continuity of theory depends. What this means is that building an architectural theory depends as much upon allowing for a reworking of the nature of theory as it does on insisting on the particularity of the architectural.

While it need not be the case that vision refers to an ideal object, it may be taken as referring to a site which is given a singular or unified nature. As such what arises is the necessity to take up the time of such an object. What is meant by this particular intrusion of time is both the way in which the object is able to be historical and thus the way in which it works to sustain the inception of its being historical. There are many different permutations that occur here. Working within most of them is the recognition that theory must address the essential, assuming that the essential is unified in nature. Here the essential is either at hand and is thus already present in any instantiated form; or the essential is not at hand and thus must be uncovered within complex determinations that mark out the present. It is this latter sense that informs Heidegger's treatment of the architectural. The distinction he draws in *Building Dwelling Thinking* between 'todays housing shortage' (*der heutigen Wohnungsnot*) and what he describes elsewhere in the same text as 'the proper plight of dwelling' (*die eigentliche Not des Wohens*) maintains and depends upon a conception of the essential that is not at hand and thus which must be uncovered.[8] The recovery of a founding propriety generates one specific philosophical and architectural task. What happens once it is assumed that all there can be is the 'housing shortage' is that the possibility of propriety has vanished. Not just the Heideggerian sense of the authentic but by extension authenticity itself. The move, however, is to the other possibility given by Heidegger's formation of the essential. In other words, the reduction of architecture to building turns architectural questions into a mere concern with what is at hand and therefore into a type of empiricism.

The switch that occurs in this instance is to that situation in which architecture did not have to engage with any particular formulation of the essence. Where this leave the activity of architecture is with a theoretical position that is only concerned with the pragmatics of building. Building, within such a set up, would have to be understood as the effect of a practice rather than as the consequence of architecture. As an effect this result mirrors the position that arises once unmasterability is equated with the impossibility of a critical or disruptive architecture. In this case, however, it would be the failure to link architectural practice to repetition and thus to the movement of historical time that lead to the abandoning of architectural thinking. Returning to the need for thinking means returning the question of the essence to history. Here, of course, history is not just that which is given by periodization and dates but the already given nature of what determines the place of activity. History is the place of the present. The present frames the question of the essence once the history of the essential has been subdued. The present becomes the site of architecture's work.

It is vital to be clear here. There is no attempt to argue against the essence as though the essential were merely that which gave itself in terms of singularity and unity. The essential needs to be recovered from precisely that conception in which singularity and unity dominated the way it came to be formulated. In such a move the essential would be pluralized. Though, again, the question concerns the nature of the plurality. The same point can be made in relation to propriety or authenticity – recall Heidegger's use of the term '*eigentliche*' – in the precise sense that arguing against the sense of propriety given by Heidegger to dwelling is not to argue against authenticity and thus by extension for a fall into inauthenticity. Once their reciprocity is noted then the shift that occurs is a distancing of *that* in terms of which the Heideggerian distinction is thought. Furthermore, arguing against a specific form of the proper – the proper within Heidegger's formulation of the 'proper plight of dwelling' – is not then to identify dwelling with the empirical presence of houses and therefore with the literal presence of buildings. What emerges is an opening up of the question of the essential. Here, an important connection emerges between the essential and the necessity of maintaining that conception of identity as identity-in-conflict. The direct consequence of this is that it becomes pointless to identify (or not to identify) the place of the architectural within the practice of philosophy as already specific and thus as formally determined, because such a move must already presupposes the fixed identity of each. In other words, the question that endures concerns how identity is to be thought rather than the assumption of identity. The pragmatics of identity have not been precluded. What they demand is a return to identity as a question.

It is in terms of such a conception of identity – delimited by the structure and temporality of the question – that it will become possible to return to the detail of Blanchot's opening formulations concerning contradiction and equally to understand why he ends the passage with the assertion that whatever is involved in such a complex set-up 'it is not a question of dialectics'. What emerges from having dealt with other responses to the 'sick tooth' – one of melancholia and the other that hovers between a singular essence or the reversion to the activity of the pragmatics of building – is that they fail to engage with the questioning that the tooth's presence occasions. In other words, the tooth holds open two important and in the end interrelated consider-ations. The first is the presence of a fissure always already inscribed within the attempt to complete. The other is the possibility of being able to reformulate the problem of appearance such that what emerges is an architecture of the incomplete. The latter affirms what Blanchot has already identified as an 'absence of dialectics'.

The absence of dialectics, the positing of a contradiction without an envisaged 'conciliation' generates neither lament nor a dramatic search for the essence, where the latter is an adventure guided by the dictates of metaphysics. On the contrary, it involves a return to the presence of time. While this may seem an arbitrary injunction – after all what would time be here – it is clear that time works these two other possibilities. Melancholia demands the attempted recovery or the overcoming of loss. It demands, in other words, the gradual effacing of that particular form of the present in order that the consequences of loss can be changed and that a type of recovery can be planned. Here architecture would have to be implicated in a form of social healing. As such there would be no attempt to take up the problem-atic presence of loss as an architectural possibility. In its place would be the long term attempt to efface the presence of this conception of loss with an architecture that obliterated its need by the counter force of renewal; a spiritual renewal. Furthermore, the purported oscillation – a movement held and articulated by the logical structure of an either/or – between a unitary essence and what would be presented as the pure pragmatics of building, is implicated in an additional oscillation. Here it is between a process of recovery that effaces the present – note after all Heidegger's use of the term '*heute*' (*der heutigen Wohnungsnot*) in the opposition between the everyday and the authentic or proper – and the positing of a more primordial time. What would define the latter is that it is a time outside the time of the everyday. The primordial and the everyday are held therefore in a reciprocity where the identity of one arises out of its opposition to the other.

It is possible therefore in the light of these identifications to return to the position established by Blanchot between 'mastery' (a mastery involving work) and the presence of a slipping away of calculation and production and thus the effect – though equally the affect – of another form of absence. Rather than a formation there is the groundlessness of formation; the form of a generative formlessness. While the detail of this position cannot be pursued here – and this because rather than pursue it in the abstract it would need the continual presence of specific architectural practices – once the generative is thought outside of an inexorable teleology of construction, then the *arché* no longer has its absolute hold on the tectonic.[9] What become important are not just looser relations and anexact connections, but their relation to programme and appearance.

In order to proceed it is vital to rescue this possibility of a generative formlessness from a series of distancing manoeuvres that would move between the charge of obfuscation on the one hand and the accusation of irrelevance on the other. What after all do these difficult and paradoxical formulations have to do with architecture no matter how the latter is thought? Without opting for too truncated a response to this question the answer hinges, as an opening, on how the negative is to be understood. In the case of the ostensibly literary this question is not as difficult as it seems. When Blanchot is writing about Mallarmé, in attempting to explicate what he describes as 'the work of absence' (*la travail de l'absence*) (135), he articulates the productive power of the negative in the following terms. It is a passage that has already been noted; '... when there is nothing, it is the nothing that can no longer be denied. which affirms, affirms again, calls the nothings as being, the unworking of being (*le désouvrement de l'etre*).[10]

In *L'expérience intérieure* Bataille in the digression on poetry defines the latter as the move from the known to the unknown. The sacrifice of the referent and the expectation of usage occur in a relentless drive towards the yet to be defined. This is the space of the literary. Sacrifice and thus poetry are opposed within Bataille's writings to the law, to morality, in sum to what he describes as 'project'. And yet the opposition is not absolute, in the same way as '*désouvrement*' is operative and thus present as workful within work, poetry understood as the negative, the power of the unknown will demand its own presentation and its being present within words, within the very words that are the place of 'project'. Bataille articulates this position with great precision: 'The plan of moral is the plan of project. The contrary of project is sacrifice. Sacrifice takes on the form of project but only in appearance.'[11]

These two moments, one in Blanchot and the other in Bataille, working with a concern for the literary reach beyond themselves. They call attention to that which is at work within and thus what brings about – works – the possibility of presentation itself. In this context this has two direct consequences; consequences, it should be added, that are precisely what the passage intends. The first is the impossibility of pure destruction; the nihilistic gesture that is also found in the promulgation of complete fragmentation. Equally, however, it opens up the possibility of defining alterity in terms of an engagement with a reworking of appearance. The questions arising here not only concern what is meant by appearance but whether or not the presence of poetry or sacrifice mediates appearance. In the latter case appearance would no longer be mere appearance. There is a final moment that is essential before returning to what here will be the ostensibly architectural.

In Derrida's *Khora* his opening concern is the productive potential of a space without space; a place without an automatic and thus autonomous site, i.e. the site of *khora*. Its importance concerns its effect on what is produced and thus the overall estimation of that production. Having already cited and worked through the opposition between logos and mythos Derrida asks,

how is one to think the necessity of that which, while giving place (*donnant lieu*) to that opposition as to so many others, seems sometimes to be itself no longer subject to the law of the very thing which it situates. What of this place? (*Quoi de ce lieu?*) It is nameable?[12]

Here it would be vital to work through the detail of Derrida's own text; tracing, perhaps, its effect within contemporary architectural practice. At this stage however the questions that arise concern the structural effect of *khora*. What is the relationship between the oppositions to which it gives rise and *khora*? Is the only appearance of *khora* the oppositions that dominate the tradition of philosophy or will there be another way of thinking that relation? Finally, is *khora* just one? Is there the possibility that in any site there will be a plethora of *khora*? In the first instance what these questions refer to is the risk that endures with any attempt to rethink the *arché* or to find another generative principle; even one detailing the power of the negative. The risk is that all that will have taken place in such a move is merely replacing one productive or generative moment with another. The problem is appearance. Will appearance be the same? What is an appearance? It is at the precise point that the literary, the philosophical and the architectural coincide. What marks the site will demand attention be paid both to the specificity of architecture as well as the specificity of the others.[13]

What resists any type of generalisation is the question of appearance. Once appearance is no longer held within a set of structuring oppositions any response to questions concerning appearance will always be constrained by particularity. Appearance is not reducible to more empirical presence, nor is it to be distanced in the name of a transcendent quality. What appears involves the constant interplay of material presence and a productive or generative dimension marked by the inevitability of a certain immateriality. Incorporated within the interplay of the material and the immaterial – articulated in terms of the retained presence of the incomplete – particularity becomes a complex and multiple site. Complexity and multiplicity yield the site of judgment.

While there has been the continual attempt to interarticulate the body and the urban this is either done through a process of abstraction or the production of coherent totalities, the more emphatic relation would occur once both locations were taken as already sites of multiple investments, different speeds and times, plural determinations all of which cohered in the same location. Here the idea of sameness while appearing spatial – after all the initial formulation of any site would been its spatial coordinates – is in fact temporal. What becomes fundamental is the recognition that the force of plurality is given by the constituent parts cohering in their difference at the same time. Here the complexity in question does not lend itself to a single view. As such theory will not accompany the object. The object does not give itself to be seen except as a complex that resists the totality of any purported optical immediacy. This state of affairs has little to do with size.

Writing of Berlin, writing it should be remembered in the 1960s, Blanchot evokes the significance of the wall in the following terms:

> the reality of the wall was destined to throw into abstraction the unity of the big city full of life, a city that was not and is not, in reality ... a single city, not two cities, not the capital of a country, not any important city, not the centre, nothing but this absent centre. In this way, the wall succeeded in concretizing abstractly the division, to render it visible and tangible, and thus to force us to think henceforth of Berlin, in the very unity of its name, no longer under the sign of a lost unity, but as the sociological reality constituted by two absolutely different cities.[14]

The collapse of the Wall, its destruction by the citizens of Berlin, did it overcome this sociological reality – two cities – or did it cause Berlin to be become the exemplary city insofar as the act of unification divided it again? No longer would the divide be in the middle. The division would be the inscription of a complex space that characterizes the city within this stage of modernity. It would be possible to continue this reworking of Blanchot's engagement with Berlin, in order to argue that what appeared as clear cut divisions now pertain at one and the same time. Moreover, it would insist on the unmasterability of a space whose complexity is sustained by time but which is held within an ontological and existential irreducibility. As such it would be possible to have come full circle. Instead of exiling division, the city would become home once it was allowed that the diaspora was already there within its confines. Allowing home, allowing as home the diasporization of the urban, and the city, is to allow the productive potential

6

LINES OF WORK

ON DIAGRAMS AND DRAWINGS

Lines and diagrams would seem to be distinct. Even though the line may work within the diagram, each retains its own specificity. On one level the distinction is clear. And yet, the distinction has an identifiable ground. What holds it in place is the field of representation. There is a coincidence of a number of apparently distinct terms once representation determines particularity. This is not to suggest that line, diagram, plan, etc. are not different but rather that the ground of the difference is the pervasive sameness enjoined by representation. Evidence of that sameness is the identification of what is taken to be a relatively unproblematic move from 'modes of representation to the actual building'.[1] Perhaps the most significant consequence of this position is that it is only with the enforced abeyance of representation, understood as that which determines their field of operation, that the real particularity of the diagram and the line would then be able to emerge. It is in light of this possibility that there will be the demand for a certain limit. The important point is not simply the problematic status of representation within architecture but that allowing representation centrality precludes any real consideration being given to the diagram as a field of experimentation. The hold of representation demands its abeyance once centrality is to be given to the particularity of the line or diagram. Allowing for this identification of the specific will take place in this instance in terms of tracing the consequences for the line and the diagram once the possibility of experimentation is introduced. A beginning can be made therefore by allowing the retained centrality representation – retained only in order to plot its limits – to confront the possibility of experimentation.

The opening question must be the following: Is there a link between the line and the diagram, and the possibility of experimentation? The immediate answer must be that there is not. Lines and diagrams, once they are assumed to represent cannot sustain experimentation in their own terms. By definition a representation always refers to what it represents. What this formulation entails is that lines and diagrams are held within a relation where their identity and status is determined by what they are not. Moreover, the realization or instantiation of what they represent needs to be understood as a form of completion. In regards to the work of lines and diagrams to the extent that either is articulated within the framework of representation and the envisaged necessity of forms of completion, experimentation is precluded. Were a line or diagram to become experimental sites then – excluding the insistence of the pragmatic – they can no longer be representations since they would have given up that determining hold in which identity is determined by a relation to an outside. Consequently, answering the opening question concerning the possible relation between lines, diagrams and experimentation in the affirmative necessitates a reformulation of both line and diagram. In the place of the complete there has to be the incomplete. The latter is not the mere negation of completion. In fact another type of completion has to emerge. The incomplete signals the possibility of the continual reworking and opening up of lines or diagrams. The presence of the space of experimentation arises when neither is taken as complete in itself. The abeyance of completion marks the limits of representation. (It also marks the point at which representation can be reintroduced. Now, it would be present as an effect of the diagram rather than the diagram being taken as a representation. The presence of representation is not taken though in terms of a simple either/or.) The limit of representation and the injunction of the incomplete is not to be interpreted as a form of failure. Rather, it is the inscription of the reality of a productive negativity within the field opened by both the line and the diagram. These notes are an attempt to sketch some of the issues at work in such a possibility.[2]

CLOSING LINES

The line already marks a space, marks it out by dividing and creating space. And yet, a line neither draws nor plots of necessity. The diagram need neither present nor hold to the spatial possibilities of something other than itself. Nor for that matter do lines and diagrams exist as ends in themselves. There may be a possibility other than that demanded by the literal. However, the history of the line as representing, as standing for, and thus as acting out, is there at the posited origin of painting. The origin as a question should not be taken as bringing considerations of truth into play; as though there were a truth about the nature of the line that comes to show itself through a concern with the origin. Rather the origin – the question of the origin – works to stage the emergence of different beginnings. Why, then, begin with the origin? The answer to the question is straightforward. However, the response does not lie in the demonstration that any origin is only ever putative and therefore not an origin at all. The aporia of the origin is not the issue. What is of interest is the conflict concerning the origin. Origins – and there will always be different and incompatible origins – stage different possibilities.

Pliny's account of the origin of painting explains the first mark in terms of the drawing of a line that holds as present – and thus *will* hold as present – that which is absent. While his text, as he indicates, is not directly concerned with establishing the origin, he nonetheless suggests that amongst the Greeks there was little disagreement that painting 'began with tracing in outline round a man's shadow' (*Natural History*, XXXV, v. 14). The drawing of the line as the origin of painting links the line to the work of representation. In addition, it opens up the way the line is more generally understood. However, representation rather than being seen as an end itself is more nuanced and is therefore more detailed. Representing, the activity of re-presentation, stages an opening articulated in terms of oppositions. The opening is already there in Pliny's formulation. At the origin, between the shadow and the figure there is an opening. One is not the other. The shadow marks the presence of what it is not. This opening has particularity since the shadow also posits a closure to the extent that the shadow is interpreted as the immediate presence of the one who cast the shadow. (The only mediation has to do with time. Allowing for, even suggesting, immediacy, is, of course, the fantasy within representation. As fantasy, and thus as the mark of a certain desire, immediacy is already mediated.)

The shadow differentiates itself and yet the act of differentiation allows for an identification – perhaps a reidentification – of that which originally cast the shadow. With the absence of the one who cast the shadow the opening is then reinforced, while the closure envisaged. Representation defines opening in terms of closure. One has to be though in relation to the other. There is an ineliminable interdependence within representation. The presence of this relation pertains to the extent that the line is defined in terns of representation rather than representation emerging as a type of effect.

In this context therefore closure refers to the demands made by the incorporation of the line, diagram, etc., into the structure of representation. Within that structure a line marks both itself and what it is not. A diagram envisages a realization in which the envisaged object is what the diagram is taken to represent. Instantiation or realization would then close the openings which are themselves already present if either the line or diagram is taken to represent. Lines and diagrams, from this perspective, work within the interdependence of absence and closure.[3]

While absence predominates, the closure is still posited insofar as the line now tracing and marking the absent figure, presents that figure and thus allows for its reidentification. With reidentification a closure is effected even though it is a closure tinged with loss precisely because closure is impossible if thought as absolute. What this particular story of the origin stages therefore, is a relationship between line and shadow in which there is a founding opening. The line endures holding a relation to the one who has gone. It is as though there is an inescapable doubling of loss. In more general terms therefore representation brings an opening for which a subsequent closure is necessarily envisaged. Openings and closures are interarticulated with the enforcing work of absence. (As always, it is an absence given to be overcome.) Fundamental to this formulation is the retention of the interplay between absence and its overcoming. What this interplay allows however is a distinction to be drawn between two different conceptions of absence. In the first place there would be absence and its overcoming as marking the work of representation; representation as re-presentation. The hyphen signalling both the presence of absence and its envisaged overcoming. On the other hand there is another sense of absence. Absence would refer to the retention of the incomplete. Within architecture the instantiation of the incomplete could then be thought in terms of Bataille's conception of the 'informe' or to utilize the psychoanalytic work of Abraham and Torok as the 'crypt'.

While the detail cannot be pursued here the important point is that absence would no longer be formulated in terms of a loss to be overcome.[4]

Working within the structure of representation the openings at work in representation's formulation occur in different sites. Representation is always more complex than a simple oscillation between presence and absence. Each site involves the effective presence of a specific type of opposition. In general these oppositions are formulated in terms of a distance to be traversed. (The oppositions both overlap and implicate each other.) The oppositions presence/absence, model/real object, plan/building, for example, instantiate a specific desire and thus specific forms of operation. The desire is the possibility that one side of the opposition holds and presents what the other side either is or will be.

At the origin of painting the image of the one who is absent has to be the actual likeness of the absent one. The image has to stand for that which is not there. It has to present it and therefore the image has to be its re-presentation. In the case of the model/real object opposition, the model will have to have become the real object. The plan becomes the building. (Thereby securing the position of model and plan as always other than the object but only after the event.) Plan and model stand for what is absent but only on the condition that presence is possible. The dictates of representation are such that movement across the divide defines activity. Moreover, it defines the way either side of the opening are to be interpreted. In other words, it is not just that representation determines the way the line, plan or diagram are to be understood, it also demands that the completed object be construed as their instantiation. That this is the interpretive set up is evident from the predominant question stemming from the presence of the divide; a divide that has to be understood as the opening within representation and thus which also functions as the source of representation. The question that each opening sets in play concerns how the divide is to be crossed; how, that is, is the opening to be closed? This question is already marked by a form of necessity. Once the line or diagram are given with the structure of representation then this question is ineliminably present. It presents that version of the incomplete that is determined, again of necessity, by the need or desire for completion. What cannot be sanctioned is the incomplete taken as an end in itself. This latter sense of the incomplete cannot be located therefore outside the object. The space given by the movement of completion – the movement between diagram and building for example – no longer provides the site of the incomplete. Once taken as internal to the object – the object as already complete and thus completed with the possible internal inscription of the incomplete – the incomplete can be understood as part of the building's actual structuration and thus as integral to the building's economy. Once located within the object the incomplete maintains itself as work.

None the less, responding to the demand for closure is, as has already been intimated, to turn the plan, drawing, model or the line into that which can only be explained within the structure of representation. It should not be forgotten that this structure allows for its own negative instance; namely a series of drawing, models, plans etc. whose interest is determined by the claim that they have purely presentational force. They could, for example, be taken as either fantastic possibilities or utopian projections. In both these instances the fantasy or the futural projection would have been identified from within the structure of representation. They present re-presentation's other possibility; namely its impossibility. As such, undertakings of this type remain on one side of the opening. Gesturing to the impossibility of the realization of the desire for completion they become representation's negative instance. Impossibility, within this formulation, is no more than the negative instance of possibility. One is defined in relation to the other. What this means is that the possibility of retrieving the line, of allowing the diagram another possibility is not be interpreted within the terms set by representation's positive or negative dimensions.

REPRESENTATION – MELANCHOLIC SPACES

Representation stages its own limits. In order to chart them it is of fundamental importance to allow representation to dictate both positive and negative instances. The reason for this importance is linked to the description, already given, of the divide that has to be crossed and which forms, from within the interpretive purview of representation, an integral part of an account of either plan, drawing or diagram. A plan marks out what is going to be present. What this means is that representation dictates that the plan or the diagram hold that absent presence in place. There is therefore a certain futurity inscribed in the existence of the plan or diagram. Futurity always points beyond. Consequently, the future is not a condition of the present, such that the future could have been inscribed in that which is present. Rather, the future is opened, demanded, because of a lack – a lack necessitating an envisaged completion – that characterizes presence. It is precisely this particular determination that is at work in the suggestion that the origin of painting is linked to the outline of that which is necessarily absent. Impossibility does not check representation, it is explained by it. Allowing for this particular formulation of the possibility of impossibility is to reiterate the work of absence and thus to delimit the diagram or plan as a melancholic space. Such an eventuality is the potential within representation.

It is essential to add here that the introduction of melancholia is intended to identify the way that representation demands a particular conception of that which demands completion. The demand is inescapable. Moreover it is precisely this demand that underlies what has already been identified as the coincidence of line, diagram and plan within the determining structure of representation.

The place of absence and with it the forced retention of this melancholic place marks what can be described as the limit of representation. Limit here is not that which is problematic within representation; it is not representation's own aporetic possibilities. The identification of limits pertains to propriety and hence to what is proper to representation once it is taken as defining the status of the diagram or line. Here, what is of primary concern is the opening and hence the link between line, drawing and diagram and a pervading sense of absence. What absence signals is the interpretive demand. As has already been intimated, what that means in this context is that the site of interpretation is marked by what it is not. This quality – the *what it is not* – needs to be linked to the future. The 'what it is not' is connected to the 'what it will be'. Melancholia predominates in the precise sense that the site itself is marked by loss – at the present, for the future – even though the object of loss, what it is that has been lost, cannot be specified in its own terms. (The lack of specificity has to do, for the most part, with the nature of the difference between the media in which the present and the future are staged.)

This definition of the site – the determination of the site as given through loss – has a number of interrelated consequences. There are two that are central. The first concerns the particularity of the line, drawing, plan, etc. Loss means that a fundamental part of their particularity stems from the *what it is not*. The subsequent realization, be it reidentification or building, reinforces the ascription of loss. The second consequence refers to the way either the line or the diagram is to be interpreted. These two consequences are related insofar as what arises with the second are the results of definitions that involve no more than simple negations. What has to be taken up – here in outline – is that which emerges once there is the departure from this structure of negation. In the place of the enforcing hold of loss – with its always possible turn to lament – there is another possibility. Loss loses its melancholic hold to become an original loss and thus a sustained founding state of the incomplete. And, as has already been intimated, what this entails is a conception of the incomplete understood not just as always already incomplete but as necessarily given within its own economy. Once the incomplete is viewed as a mark of production then the incomplete brings with it its own generative capacity. As will be suggested it is precisely this possibility that arises in the move from a formulation of the ontological in terms of stasis to a conception determined by the centrality of becoming. However, it has to be a conception of becoming that retains the movement to form. There cannot be pure process without that movement. With mere becoming form is precluded and therefore the architectural is continually deferred. Allowing form as interarticulated with movement and therefore with the centrality of becoming is, as will be suggested, the potential within Leibniz's theory of the monad.

Rather than cross the divide and thus rather than allow the desire to cross the divide and unify what would otherwise have been an opposition to determine the structure within which the line or diagram is to be understood, another possibility emerges. It arises to the extent that negation is fundamentally reworked in terms of the incomplete.

Here it is essential to be clear. The distance being staged here is from a structure in which there is an envisaged movement from the presentation of what is yet-to-be – thereby defining that presentation as the representation of what it is not – to the subsequent realization or instantiation of that earlier representation. What this means is that given the demands of this structure the yet-to-be comes to be completed. Within this set up, the site defined in term of negation (and which allows for the ascription of melancholia precisely because it is defined in terms of loss) both envisages and demands its own subsequent negation. In other words, the incomplete demands to be completed; loss insists on its own overcoming. Allowing for another conception of the incomplete cannot be given within the opposition incomplete/complete. Alterity cannot be defined as the mere affirmation of a different terms within an either/or. The incomplete has to maintain itself as such. Maintaining here is necessarily interarticulated with production. It is this position that has to be developed.[5]

LINES OF WORK

Representation is defined in terms of a certain conception of negation. Allusion has already been made to this conception in terms of the 'what it is not'. Within this formulation the diagram, the line, are what they are because they allow for their instantiation in a form other than their own; they allow for a completion in a time (the future) that is not their own. Having been completed – completed in the sense of having been instantiated – both the line and the diagram are necessarily devoid of possibilities. They lose their capacity for investigation or research. This does not just mean that the possibility for experimentation is linked to the incomplete, but that experimentation needs to allow what had been taken to be representations to sustain a generative quality and therefore to allow interpretations beyond the hold of representation. Within the strictures characterizing the operation of representation – moving as it must from the incomplete to the complete and thus from the present to the future – this quality is denied because line, diagrams and plans are taken as demanding their own completion and thus of having been completed. (Again, it is essential to allow for the coincidence of plans, diagrams and lines within representation.) What predominates here is a conception of negation that is linked to its own overcoming through the act of completion (either real or envisaged). Neither the truth nor the viability of this set up comprise what is central to this position. Centrality has to be given to the demand for the act of completion. Realization precludes experimentation precisely because it is the mark of this act of completion; or at least that is the demand that is made.

There is a twofold movement at work here. Representation denies that either the line or the diagram could present possibilities resisting completion. Moreover, to the extent that either were allowed to have this capacity, then neither the line nor the diagram could be interpreted within the determinations given by the work of representation. How then does it become possible to account for the work of lines and the field of activity given by the diagram? Answering this question still demands working through the given determinations of representation.

The term haunting the structure of representation, haunting it precisely because it defines its most essential determination, is melancholia. Representation is marked by loss. However what is absent cannot be named as such; moreover it cannot be readily identified. The desire of representation is for that which completes it and thus, with this desire, what is given in the re-presentation is the lost object. Representation insists on a completion that it cannot identify as absolute. It is tempting to suggest therefore that it is always ruined in advance. Here melancholia works with the ruin of completed form. Taken as the defining term loss restricts activity by limiting the range of work.

There is however another ruin. Neither ruined in advance nor the ruined form of what already stood. Beyond the strictures of the melancholic turn there is the ruin that yields form. (A ruin that will have already freed itself from the hold of the literal.) It is not the ruin of form but the ruin that forms. This ruin demanding the abeyance of any problematics of loss is the diagram or the line once freed from the need to represent. What this means is that rather than open out by trying to stand for what they are not, the line and diagram open up within themselves. Allowing for the continuity of this opening, allowing for the continuity of an opening resisting absolute finality and thus an enforcing completion, is to allow for both line and diagram to take on the status of plural events.[6] Plurality here does not refer to the domain of meaning where plurality would be mere semantic overdetermination. Rather, for the diagram or the line to take on this status they would become the site of an ontological irreducibility. They would, for example, articulate the determinations of the Leibnizian monad once its demands were drawn. Moreover, it is in terms of the monad that representation as an effect can be reintroduced. The monad allows for representation – working beyond the hold of loss – precisely because it is not formulated and articulated within a structure of representation.

For Leibniz, within the general structure of argument presented the The Monadology the monad always presents itself and can be perceived as such in a particular form at a particular time. None the less, the monad is always more than this formal actuality. And yet the 'more' is not derived from links to the monad. On the contrary, it is internal to the monad itself. Leibniz formulates this in terms of the 'principle of change' being internal to the monad. The monad 'is' – is itself – in its continual opening up within itself. It plots and replots itself. It could not be described as the continuity of an opening without end unless there were the fundamental recognition that the monad is, at the same time, an endless opening always having a particular form. The monad is the copresence of continuity and discontinuity; of form and the generation of form; of instantiation and becoming. With the monad these terms are taken as coexisting and therefore not as mutually exclusive. Presentation is always an effect of an economy of production. As an economy – a production of endless completion opened by the effective presence of the incomplete – it allows the monad to become the diagram. While it would necessitate a more sustained engagement with Leibniz that can be developed here what has to be taken up are the possibilities – initially the ontological and temporal possibilities – inherent in the formulation of the monad as 'multiplicity in unity'. With this move, one that in general terms is occasioned by the diagram having the ontological status of a plural event, it becomes the site of experimentation. The diagram is the place of a mapping and remapping in which finitude is always an effect of an ineliminable infinite.

In part, what this means, can only be understood once it is recognized that the diagram and the line are not the representation of 'multiplicity in unity'. The diagram cannot be taken as re-presenting this set up. Quite simply, there cannot be a re-presentation of complex relations where complexity involves both ontological and temporal considerations. They can only be enacted. The diagram, in order to maintain itself as the site of experimentation, has to work with that possibility. When Leibniz, in the same text, refers to the 'infinite folds of the soul', it is not as though there could have been an accompanying drawing detailing that infinity. The infinite in that instance involves the demand to think the relationship between the finite and the infinite such that a cross-section would map that relation. The monad – perhaps also the 'soul' – once formulated in terms of a founding and ineliminable plurality, therefore as plural events, raise the question of their own presentation. Reading the diagram as a plural event therefore, is not to read it as a monad, or even as a site containing the soul's 'infinite folds' since such an approach would be too literal.

Rather, what has to be retained is the question of economy. Experimentation, understood as the opening freedom at work once the hold of representation is in abeyance, is the co-presence of the complete and the incomplete. It is not as though there is a representation of that relation. The diagram must always be completing. Any pragmatic instance – and it is necessary to redefine the pragmatic in relation to the process of completing – must figure within and thus figure that process. This complex process of possible and actual inter-relations set the conditions within which lines and diagrams are to be read. What is read therefore is the line at work.

The pragmatic occurrence is the possibility of a reintroduction of representation. It can occurs in two ways. The first occurs in an act of rereading. What defines the act is the interpretive refusal to read that which was taken to be simply representational as a mere representation. The second is more productive and more closely linked to the question of experimentation. While it can be argued that the diagram as presented above is not itself a representation in the strict sense of the term, this does not preclude the possibility that at certain points or at certain moments elements of the diagram can be attributed a representational quality. Such an attribution would be pragmatic and strategic. As such representation and thus the capacity to represent become effects of the diagram rather than the diagram's architectural extension. In addition, freeing the diagram from the hold of representation, though allowing representation to be present as a possible effect, opens up as both as a theoretical question as well as an architectural one, how the move from the diagram to plan and section is to be thought and therefore enacted. If the diagram is taken as purely representational then such a move is already determined in advance. Once the diagram is attributed a different status then areas of inquiry and indeed areas of experimentation emerge as given within the gap between diagram and plan and section.

Two points need to be made in conclusion. The first reiterates what has already emerged, while the second opens up a domain for further consideration. Both need the setting of the work of lines and diagrams within the possibility of experimentation within architecture. In this first instance, once freed from the need to represent, the line and the diagram work as ends in themselves. This is not intended to preclude pragmatic necessities, rather it is to allow for the emergence of the diagram as plotting a complexity – a complex of relations – that is always more than the addition of elements. The conception of complexity at work here is the movement of realization occasioned by the lines in question but which the lines cannot be taken as representing. At that moment the diagram emerges freed from its original need to present what is not there. What this means is that the diagram can inscribe the future into the present because that possibility is itself part of the present's own self-constitution. The second points opens up a further limit. If within the diagram lines are given different weightings such that speed and time define the presence of the line – a geometry of movement rather than that of mere place – then the intersection of two lines, while appearing in any diagram as the intersection of those lines, will always have been more. The nature of the intersection as a staged irreducibility defined in terms of time and speed marks the impossibility of interpreting the diagram within the structure of representation. The diagram works within itself allowing a continual reworking within the incorporation of different weightings. Diagrams and lines stage that work and therefore are able to be redefined in terms of lines of work.

PART III

BODY, PLACE AND HISTORY

INTRODUCTION

Memory and its place and possibility in architecture have become and still endure as insistent architectural problems. While not attempting to equate them – to do so would diminish their force – the collapse of Eastern Europe and the continual effects of the Holocaust have had a direct impact upon the question of how architecture remembers. Of the many dangers inherent in pursuing this topic one of the most prevalent is to make memory an abstract question and therefore to think that it is always the same problem. Abstraction is even possible in regards to the Holocaust. In this context it inheres in the position that the treatment by film, or by literature or by architecture, for example, can be conflated because their subject matter is the same. Literature's engagement with questions of memory while not itself unified none the less differs in important ways from architecture's engagement. The same will be true of film in relation to literature and architecture. Accounting for these differences necessitates recognizing that a different medium is involved in each instance.

Chapter 8 arose out of a conference held in Bucharest. The conference while academic in nature was directly concerned with Ceaucescu's architectural legacy. One of the immediate problems was that he had created his vision of Bucharest by destroying most of what had been there before. While there were pockets that remained, in most instances even the traces of the past had been obliterated. There were two architectural and philosophical questions that the legacy posed: How is destruction to be understood? Could the consequences of destruction be destroyed or would that amount to simple reiteration of the founding problem? That these are theoretical question – in the sense of the term theoretical that has already been developed – is self-evident in so far as they cannot be thought other that in relation to the architectural setting from which they flow. The problem of Bucharest has already been addressed in Chapter 3 in relation to Reiser and Umemoto's work. Here, rather than a specific project providing the analysis, it stems from developing a response to the twofold question of destruction posed above. Working through Descartes's conjoining of the philosophical and the architectural in order that he take up the relationship between destruction and the new provides the way into the problem.

Chapter 9 is specifically concerned with issues raised by Holocaust. The problem posed is simple. The question it yields is stark. How not to forget? The answer to this question does not reside in the making of one particular architectural form that will resolve the problem by always precluding forgetting and occasioning remembrance. Beginning to address the question involves a twofold recognition. The first is that remembering – i.e. both remembering and not forgetting – demands that the monument be such that it resists automatic assimilation. Assimilation will occasion disappearance and thus forgetting. Taken as a metaphor assimilation becomes a form of absolution. The second element is that intrinsic to any attempt to take up the problem of remembrance necessitates an engagement with the problem of historical time. To remember by resisting assimilation is already the commitment to that view of historical time that works against simple continuity and thus works contrary to the position that identifies historical time with the inexorable march of chronology. A march which in incorporating the 'all' of history reduces that content to a simplified repetition of Sameness.

The question of time is fundamental to any understanding of architecture. The same is true in regards to historical time. The question of the future as simple projection and thus as unthought outside the vicissitudes of chronology informs the conception of the future in the film *Blade Runner*. This film has had an important effect on the study of architecture. Here rather than approaching it in terms of the purely architectural, allowing it to remain a film, poses the question of the relationship between architecture and film. Any engagement with its vision of architecture – particularly the architecture of the future – has to maintain that context. It is at its most effective when its archi-

7

HOUSING THE FUTURE

THE ARCHITECTURE OF
BLADE RUNNER

Where is the future? How will it be built? One way of taking up these questions would be to follow the presentation of the architectural within films that seek to project the future. The copresence of the two – the architectural within film – brings two interrelated constraints into play. The first pertains to film; to its being a medium of representation. In this instance it is the medium itself that works to constrain. Secondly there will be the constraint of function. Even though the architecture of the future may differ it will have to function as architecture. Even allowing for changes within it, difference will still be mediated by the retention of function. While it is clear that function is more complex than any idealization of its presence allows, what is of overall significance here is that the copresence of these constraints marks the necessity of relation. In being necessary it will have to be thought. The primordality of relation means that what will remain as an ineliminable part of any built future is its being architecture. Equally taking film, at least initially, as a medium of representation means that the images presented within it needs to be located within a visual field. Allowing for the fact that the nature of the image may need to be reconsidered, if not reassessed, film will, nonetheless, always have to represent.

What has been identified here as constraints may seem trivial. All they are asserting is that architecture must retain its specificity and that film must work with – and within – representation. And yet despite the apparently obvious nature of these assertions their importance lies in what they identify. In the case of both their possibility lies in the necessity of a connection to the present. As such both bring with them the importance and centrality of time. In the case of architecture the difficulty of thinking its future does not lie in a lack of imagination or capacity for futural projection it is rather that the future and therefore its being thought always need to be undertaken in relation to the present and furthermore to be seen as a condition of the present. It is thus that the question of the future can always be reworked in terms of the possibility of another thinking. In the case of science fiction films the challenge that arises with them is the extent to which what they are offering either in terms of film or, in this instance in terms of architecture, amounts to that other possibility. Alterity here is always different from projected utopias. On this account the possibility of a pure utopia, a place outside of all relation is an impossibility.

Before pursuing the interplay of film and architecture in *Blade Runner* – an interplay always conditioned by the work of constraint – a third element needs to be introduced. The presence of the body – the body within the architectural body as well as within the body of the film – needs to be taken up. Not only is the body implicated in the architectural by figuring, historically, as an important metaphor or analogy for the architectural, the move away from the physical human body towards the 'replicant' or more radically towards the cyborg, positions and holds the body in another form. It is re-formed and maintained. The question hinges on what it is that is maintained and how the analogy between architecture and body is structured by this change. It may be that other bodies will have been possible once the body – the possible other body – has to bear a relation to the present. Relation here is the site of critique; it is moreover critique's condition of possibility.

Los Angeles, November 2019, is the announced setting of Ridley Scott's *Blade Runner*. Here the immediate problem is the presence on earth of Nexus 6 Replicants. This advanced form of robot had been involved in mutinies in the 'Off World'. As a consequence all replicants that manage to get back to earth are to be hunted down and then 'retired'. Blade Runner was the name given to those whose job it was to effect the retirement. The film's chronological setting, its urban location and the presence of replicants brings history (here the future), architecture (Los Angeles and the urban environment) and the body (e.g. the necessity to distinguish between replicant and human) into connection. Rather than taking this film either as programmatic or as having an exemplary status here its importance is that what it allows is a way of tracing a specific formation of these three elements. The importance of that formation is that it provides a way of thinking about the opening questions. Where is the future? How will it be built?

As the replicant is more or less indistinguishable from the human, special tests are needed or in order to establish their identity. In the case of the Nexus 6 their capacity to develop more advanced emotional responses than the previous generation of replicants made their identification even more difficult and therefore correspondingly even more urgent. The test devised by Deckard involves observing pupil dilation during a detailed questioning. Replicants will in the end identify themselves by the inability to show the same level of immediate emotional response to certain questions. Within the structure of the film the presence of the replicant allows for a general questioning of the guarantees of identity. When Deckard and Rachel first met, and before he is aware that she is a replicant, she asks Deckard whether he has 'ever retired a human by mistake?' At a later stage when she confronts him with her past – a past that in the process is truly identified as fiction – she pointedly inquires if he himself has taken his own test. In other words, the film in introducing and maintaining the possibility that Deckard may be a replicant heightens the already ambiguous replicant/human relation. The level of gene technology that produced the 'skin jobs' is not just used with humans it is also deployed in the recreation of other animals. A trip through a market reveals snakes and ostriches amongst others. The owl at Tyrell headquarters is a replicant. There is an important level of instability that is introduced and reintroduced by the presence of these animals. It is interesting to note that this is brought about not through the use of hard technology but through work with genes. DNA manipulation has enabled the replicant to be produced. Here the prosthetic is for the most part absent. Moreover the use of drugs and virtual reality that complicates the constructed space in which, for example, Marva the main character in Pat Cadigan's *Fools* finds herself is also absent. With this work the question of subjectivity is played out in terms of the human and the human's own creation. What is absent is the possible reworking and reposition of subject positions. It is this precise sense that the replicant can be distinguished from the cyborg. Donna Harraway's own description of the cyborg is worth recalling:

The cyborg is resolutely committed to partiality, irony, intimacy, innocence. No longer structured by the polarity of public and private, the cyborg defines a technological polis based partly on a revolution of social relations in the *oikos*, the household. Nature and culture can no longer be the resources for appropriation or incorporation by the other.[1]

What does the cyborg offer? The answer to this question lies in the reference to the 'household'. The question is what force can the evocation of such a house hold? Its place will be problematic. The architecture as well as interior design within *Blade Runner* is more straightforward. The police station to which Deckard is taken has an entrance area reminiscent of a large railway station – places in the American context which are already marked by a certain redundancy – while within the office the filing cabinets are wooden. The desk is conventional. The presence of fans indicates the absence or failure of air conditioning. Here technology is only partly at work. The office indicates a continuity with a certain image of the present. On the other hand the cars used by the police do not maintain the same level of continuity. They are technology at a very sophisticated level, or rather they are machines at a very sophisticated level. Technology is always used as a servant for the human. The potentially interactive space of human and machine only exists within a genetic context. Moreover it is because the relationship between human and machine is located in opposition that the replicant is able to pose such a threat and more significantly why the architecture within the film has to enact a series of almost predictable conventions. What marks out the futural dimension of the buildings?

Deckard's apartment is standard. It is not as though it enacts a yet to be determined structure of domesticity. It would be a perfect home for Rachel were she not a replicant. On one level what makes it seem unfair that they have to flee is that as a domestic setting it is ideal. And yet on another it could not be ideal as it is an architecture that could not house the consequences of her having been accepted. Accepting the replicant may demand another architecture. As a work of architecture his apartment's only concession to the future – and here would be a putative concession – is the voice activated lift and the location of his apartment on the 97th floor. While it introduces a further element of instability into the film there is the strong suggestion that the majority of the population have left and now inhabit the 'Off World'. Immigrant communities, corporate headquarters, elements of government and those who work within them seem to be all that has remained. And yet while this works to open up the question of the architecture of the other world in the end this question is otiose as there is no need to think that even there the relationship between human and technology – be that technology machine or gene based – would be any different.

The Tyrell headquarters seems to be modelled on a Mayan temple. Internally its architecture and design is eclectic. A visionary future is held at bay by size. As with the elevation of Deckard's apartment here the only concession to the future – albeit an imagined future – is given through scale. Conversely other architectural possibilities are provided by the transformation of the given. However the transformation in question is decay. What comes to be juxtaposed within the cosmo-politan urban fabric is decay – the continuity rather than the teleology of decay – and the modern vast. The replicant is seen as a threat within this context. It is at this point that the constraint governing both architecture and film need to be reintroduced.

What characterizes the replicant is its filmic possibility. Rachel, Pris, Zhora are ostensibly human. They are not stylized machines. In the case of Roy his poignant claim that he has seen and experienced more than any human almost makes him more human than the humans. It is as though he has lived at the very edge of human existence. Indeed his death – he dies by simply running out of life – seems the most quintessentially human aspiration for death. Neither killed nor fatally ill his life just runs out at the appointed time. At that moment he shows himself to be what the replicant had always been, namely an other who was never absolutely other. Robots, androids, the dolls populating J. F. Skinner's apartment – even the machine with skin – would always be purely other. Acts of differentiation would be straight-forward. Differences would proliferate and insist. The body of the replicant does not allow for complete differentiation. They are both part of the set up while not being part of it. They become therefore a mediating moment. Their filmed presence allows them to be the same, but only in the moment of their differentiation. Equally that presence allows them to be different by presenting them as the same. As body and as the analogue for architecture they are both at home and not at home.

The replicant works through the opposition of same and other by turning that opposition into an identity by incorporating it. As such the architectural aesthetic within *Blade Runner* that posits an otherness that is only explicable in terms of decay and size has done no more than heighten possibilities already present in contemporary urban life. The disruptive possibility of a relation with a replicant arises because of the recognition of the actuality of alterity. This can be worked through both in relation to the replicant itself or in terms of a necessary concession about the already divided nature of self. The architecture of the film cannot provide an architecture for replicants. That refusal – a refusal articulated within a banalized conception of architectural otherness – leaves open the question of what it would mean to be at home with replicants. Answering it must work through the analogy between architecture and body. This time however taking the replicant's body as the point of departure. Only by starting with replicants will it be possible to house cyborgs.

8

DESCARTES AND THE ARCHITECTURE OF CHANGE

Perhaps, the most remarkable legacy of the regime in Romania is the architecture of Bucharest. The complicated problem of what to do with this legacy is the address of this paper.[1] The problem is both architectural and philosophical. Repeating the destruction that created the present city by a further act of destruction is not an intervention. What must be done involves developing ways of understanding the regime's own urbanism and thus ways of countering it. Fundamental to both is thinking a conception of the new or the other which demands the abeyance of destruction on the one hand and the refusal of a nostalgic sense of recovery on the other. (The latter would be the new as the rediscovery of a lost tradition.) Approaching this issues via Descartes may seem aberrant. And yet the real strength of the Cartesian formulation of the interplay between the philosophical and the architectural is that it is premised on the interconnection between destruction and the new. The limits of Descartes therefore are central to thinking the limits of this conception of modernity.

One of the problems confronting any attempt either to present conceptually, let alone enact, fundamental change is the housing of that which occurs in the process and as the consequence of such change. While it is always essential to hold to particularity, it remains the case that this problem will endure within philosophy as much as it will within architecture. Not only must there be the possibility that change can be registered, given the impossibility of sustaining a successful link between change and either the utopian project or a metaphysics of destruction, it must also be the case that there is a form continuity. What this means is that an integral part of the problem stems from having to give formal presence to a discontinuous continuity. Within the context of the countries comprising the former Eastern Europe,

part of the challenge to be faced if the authoritarian regimes that characterized their former existences are no longer to be politically or
architecturally present, is how to house the future. (This is, of course,
a question concerning the present and not an imagined future.)

Engaging with the issues that arise demands the resources of architects, political scientists and philosophers. Philosophy is positioned by
such questions because philosophy has consistently concerned itself
with the problems of cessation and continuity, and inclusion and exclusion. Analysing the way these problems are taken up opens up differing
ways in which the interplay between change and its housed presence
can be thought. Rather than giving this problem a purely abstract
determination, it can be given setting that comes from a consideration
of the domestic and the body within the work of Descartes. The importance of this setting is that Descartes' writings bring the architectural
and the domestic within the setting of an attempt, albeit one undertaken within philosophy, to think radical change.

PHILOSOPHY AND THE DOMESTIC

Two well known motifs in Descartes' work will allow these philosophico-architectural considerations to be opened up. Descartes
reference to the possible renewal of a city and its buildings as presented
in the *Discours de la mèthod* comprises the first. The second will be
the investigation of the nature of the distinction between the human
and the animal, and the human and the machine staged by Descartes
both in the *Discours* and in the *Le Traité de l'homme*. In general
terms what emerges from an analysis of these two motifs is the insistent necessity to judge mastery or rather to judge the desire for mastery.
While the choice will not be positioned around an either/or in any
straightforward sense, it remains the case that the critique of the
conception of mastery within Descartes writings opens up the possibility of a conception of subjectivity and thus of architecture that will
be positioned around the incomplete. Rather than the incomplete being
the sign of lack, it registers the impossibility of there ever having been
the unity and thus the already present self-completion demanded by
a self-enclosing and thus self-giving conception of architecture or
subjectivity. In the place of a politics of lament there is a political –
and thus an architectural – configuration that continues to work
within and through the incomplete. Strategies of working with the

incomplete – of the always already incomplete – will, in the end, demand another form of universality and therefore another thinking of the absolute; it is an absolute allowing for anoriginal complexity. The demand would be different in so far as it would involve a founding ontology of the incomplete. What this will mean, philosophically, is that the always already incomplete is an ontological set up and not the consequence of a semantic undecidability.[2] Philosophy, and with it a philosophical thinking of architecture, will have been constituted by the ineliminable presence of the plural event.

Even though Cartesian formulation is well know it is worth allowing the detail of his position to be cited.

> there is not usually so much perfection in works composed of several parts and produced by various different craftsmen as in the works of one man. Thus we see that buildings undertaken and completed by a single architect are usually more attractive and better planned than those which several have tried to patch up by adapting old walls built for different purposes. Again, ancient cities that have gradually grown from mere villages into large towns are usually ill-proportioned, compared with those orderly towns which planners lay out as they fancy on level ground. Looking at the buildings of the former individually, you will often find as much art in them, if not more, than in those of the latter; but in view of their arrangement a tall one here, a small one there – and the way they make the streets crooked and irregular, you would say it is *chance*, rather than the will of men using *reason*, that placed them so. And when you consider that there have always been certain officials whose job it is to see that private buildings embellish public places, you will understand how difficult it is to make something perfect by working only on what others have produced.[3]
>
> (1: 519, my emphasis)

Held within these lines is an implicit conception of historical time. It defines the nature of change by providing it with its philosophical possibility. Furthermore, what characterizes this particular conception of change – indeed what would count almost as an architecture after the enactment of destruction – is that it is structured in terms of the opposition between chance and reason. It is the conception of historical time that is at work with this passage and which in turn holds in place, and is held in place by, the opposition between chance and reason, that are central. Any attempt to think the through question of change is constrained by the ineliminability of temporal concerns.

The ostensible point of Descartes's example was to indicate why it is better for a single philosopher to recast philosophy – to provide it with new foundations – than attempt to refurbish what the Scholastic tradition had given as the philosophical, and thus as that which set the conditions for truth. Employing the language of the *Meditations* what was necessary was 'destruction.' Moreover, it is an act of destruction that has to be singular in nature. Its singularity will, of course, lend itself to a necessary universalization. Reason provides the basis of universality since the act of destruction and the subsequent philosophico-architectural activity are acts of reason. The project of a new philosophy, as with that which would pertain to a new house or a new city, is not to have to work on 'what others have produced'. A real departure – be it architectural or philosophical – must involve the interplay of destruction and the new. The former being the precondition for the latter. In other words, the presence of the new is premised upon the destruction of the old.

While the full force of the Cartesian project may not have been apparent to Descartes, what must be maintained is that with Descartes there arises that version of the modernist project which works by maintaining and articulating a metaphysics of destruction. What characterizes such a metaphysics is that it is given within a destructive possibility in which alterity – an-other philosophy, architecture, etc. – arises out of a destruction of the given. Here, not only is time such that it is possible to intervene within it in order to establish the new, memory will not work against this particular construal of renewal. In the end, this position becomes more intricate, nonetheless what emerges at this stage is the opposition between destruction and memory. The latter term needs to allowed to have both its positive and negative determinations – in other words it must be allowed to be present as either remembering or forgetting. Destruction is premised on either an enforced forgetting or the attempted elimination of traces thereby trying to obviate memory's possibility.

The setting this passage is given in the text is located within what could be described as the straightforwardly domestic. Immediately prior to making this claim Descartes writes that it had occurred to him after spending the day 'shut up in a stove heated room.' In other words, the comfort of the domestic setting – a warm room within the house – determines the need to engage in an argument about philosophy and the development of philosophy which is itself advanced in terms of an analogy whose concerns touch on architecture, urbanism and forms of restoration. Moreover, the precise nature of the engagement necessitates a destruction of the edifice that comprises the philosophical tradition – as construed by Descartes – and thus, to the extent the analogy is maintained, it demands a sustained rebuilding and redevelopment on the level of the architectural. This set up has to be thought in terms of the implicit conception of temporality that inheres in the formulation of the architectural analogy.

What attention to the details of Descartes's formulation reveals is not the presence of a foundering moment within the text as such, but a complication given by the temporality proper to the analogy's own work. Inherent in it is the proposition that the time of historical development – the temporality of the philosophical tradition and equally the tradition of building – while continuous or sequential time allows for an emphatic intervention in which the content of the tradition can be destroyed and the philosophical project is able to begin again 'all anew from the foundations'. There is however one fundamental additional detail. The 'stove heated room' seems to be outside that particular formulation. Before pursuing its details the direct consequence of this positioning needs to be noted. The domestic – and here it is not just the domestic but the domestic as the site in which truth comes to be recognized – is lodged outside that domain to which truth refers. The domestic is positioned outside the city and thus as, in some sense, outside its buildings. Despite being placed outside, it comes to reveal the truth of that which takes place within the city. Furthermore what counts as the domestic can be extended in so far as the 'stove heated room' has an almost inevitable ubiquity. Most sites lend themselves to a domestic rendering. What this means is that if the domestic is the site in which the necessity for the enactment of a metaphysics of destruction has come to insist, then it is equally the site that is not included within its own reworking. Reverting to the analogy, it would be as though the 'stove heated room' was not located within the old city – and if it were to be then it would be there by chance – and thus not in need of another set of foundations.

Indeed it is possible to see that this is the position that is reinforced by the other major recourse to the language of architecture that occurs in the text. In the opening of the Third Section, Descartes argues that it is not sufficient prior to the act of rebuilding – and note his formulation is 'to rebuild the place where on lives' (1: 591) – simply to prepare for the work. It is impermissible to be *irrésolu*. This accounts for why it is essential that 'one is lodged happily during the time that the works is being carried our' (1: 591) In other words, there is a necessity to be 'lodged happily' during the time in which the philosophical project is carried out. Part of what this entails, for Descartes, is 'obeying the law and customs' of the land in which he finds himself; not only is that essential, not engaging in activity, be it philosophical or otherwise, that was not part of the project of truth or which would lead away from the pursuit of truth is equally a fundamental part of being 'lodged happily.' What cannot come into the domain of reconsideration, reexamination let alone refurbishment is the initial setting in which this activity is undertaken. If designs are to be made – if 'one' is to become the architect, again a possibility identified by Descartes, the philosopher becoming the architect – then the sanctity of the home in which these plans are made and laid out is a fundamental condition; it is almost the *sine qua non*. Perhaps, here, it is possible to argue that the exclusion of the domestic – textually the place of being 'lodged happily' – is the condition of possibility for the project of reworking the philosophical. Metaphysical destruction is constrained to leave the home intact. It will be essential to return to this point. What it sets is play is the possibility that strategies of destruction may end up conserving the place of the domestic since the home cannot be subject to the same demands as that which is outside its walls; even though, as has already been noted this is outside is there in name only.

At this point time needs to be reintroduced. What has arisen thus far is that time as it is at work within the structure of Descartes's argument must have at least two particular determinations. In the first place, it must be such that intervention is possible in order that the project of philosophy can be reworked and thus given another foundation; moreover bringing about this situation must be the work of a solitary individual: the philosopher architect. In the second place, while what appears to be public space – though in the end it will be no more that a private philosophical space – must be able to sanction this dramatic intervention, it must also be the case that what emerges as the domestic must fall outside the temporality that is, for Descartes, proper to the tradition of philosophy. What this means is that philosophy, thus conceived, is divorced from the everyday and in being divorced from it comes to yield a conception of the everyday as untouched by philosophy. The everyday and the domestic – remembering the ubiquity of the domestic – are not just removed from the domain of the philosophical. It is rather that the concept of time that pertained to the unfolding of the philosophical – a temporality allowing for intervention and thus allowing, initially at least, the determining presence of a metaphysics of destruction – is not that in which the repetition of the domestic and the everyday are repeated. (And yet, as has already been suggested, there is a certain reciprocity at work within this set up.)

The Cartesian project of renewal therefore in leaving the everyday untouched leaves its architecture untouched. While the use of architecture within the text works to indicate how a metaphysics of destruction would be enacted within philosophy – the new buildings, a new urban landscape springing from the originality of one mind at work – in the end there will be no change since the site of thinking, its home, the place in which one is 'lodged comfortably' remains outside the call for renewal. In this instance architecture conserves the everyday and the domestic as they are untouched, necessarily, by philosophy. And it must be added that it is not just that they are untouched they are equally not viewed as places warranting or needing the renewal that is demanded for philosophy by philosophy. What this means is that the place of bodies, the spatial relation that pertains between bodies and the place in which they find themselves and thus which is the locus of experience, are left out of consideration. Descartes has, of course, already made this point by withdrawing the domain of law and custom from the place of philosophical renewal. Despite the presence of the architectural within the text, despite the utilization of explicitly architectural motifs, the architectural is not thought as such. The repetition of the end of architecture – its presence in terms of a building in which sheltering take place – occurs without consideration. Or, in fact the only consideration that is offered is the form that conserves the predetermined functions that architecture has been taken to serve. The question of lodging – let alone the question of what it means to lodge well – in not being addressed, has to be assumed.

What is introduced therefore is not simply that which checks the Cartesian conception of the new, but the more demanding proposition that once the new is interarticulated with destruction then what will be left out is the place in which destruction is conceived. What this means is that what comes to be advanced is a conception of the new that will leave the customs and the laws of the domestic untouched. Once again, assuming the ubiquity of the domestic what is removed from consideration, and thus the possibility of its own renewal, is the everyday. This may have a number of different consequences. One is that the presence of architectural or urban destruction – renewal and thus the promulgation of the new as consequent on destruction undertaken in the name of the new, perhaps even in the name of progress – amounted to no more than a reiteration of the same domestic spaces, and thus the reinforcing of spaces with the same domestic politics as had existed before.

As architecture was in the end left untouched within Descartes argument, this opens up the need to search for ways in which it may be incorporated into the possibility of thinking change. Architecture may be included once it is understood as being both the locus and agent of change rather than the neutral place of being 'lodged happily'. In fact once it becomes impossible to avoid an analysis of what this state involves, what would then emerge is that the most sustained critique of forms of human activity – critiques that envisage the possibility of a type of transformation – would be critical engagements with the architecture that sustained the particular forms of activity in question.

BODIES, MACHINES AND SOULS

In order to investigate the operation of the human body and therefore as part of the attempt to establish what it was that defined the human, Descartes often used analogies with machines and invented animals which, for all intents and purposes, resembled in their actions, humans. Descartes could 'suppose' that God has formed 'the body of a man' which, even though it did not have a soul, was nonetheless of a nature such that examining its operations would amount to examining the operations of the body of a human being. Descartes's immediate concession is that the human body is also an animal body. Indeed his own justification mirrors this set up. Explaining that what he wants to establish is a link between the animal body and the human body, the link is presented in the following terms.

> I want to put here the explanation of the movement of the heart and the arteries, which, being the first and the most general that are observed in animals, it will be easy to judge on the basis of them what one must think (*ce qu'on doit penser*) of all the others.
>
> (1: 619)

The 'man' like the human except for the absence of a 'soul' ('*l'ame raisonnable*') allows claims which once generalized account, equally, for the operation of the human body. What governs this movement, indeed what allows it to have its explanatory force are resemblance and imitation. In sum, there is a generalized mimetic economy that allows for the analogy to hold.

The opening of the *Traité de l'homme* reinforces this point. Again, it begins with the supposition that the body is 'nothing other than a statue or a machine of the earth'. Investigating this other body – the body machine – will lead to an investigation of the human body since '. . . it imitates all of our functions which can be imagined to proceed from matter and which only depend upon the operation of the organs' (1: 379).

Furthermore, after a lengthy description of the operation of the body Descartes concludes that this entity – the automaton – 'imitates' perfectly the actions of man. Here, what he calls, 'this machine' is on the level of imitation indistinguishable from the human.

Now, the mimetic economy only works if it is possible to establish the moments at which the human can be distinguished from the machine or the animal. Resemblance while productive, is for Descartes, equally an important source of error. The question therefore concerns how the mimetic economy is to be disrupted such that rather than a correspondence what emerges is a necessary non-correspondence between the machine or animal and the human. Answering that question involves recognizing that the argument advanced by Descartes in the *Meditations*, and elsewhere, is concerned to link the specificity of the human to the activity of thinking and thus not to the operations of the body. Nonetheless, what has to happen is that Descartes needs to describe the activities of thinking in such a way that they are

automatically irreducible to bodily activities. It is this point that needs
to be pursued. Pursuing it is equally to question the role of the mimetic
economy in the formulation of the Cartesian position.

In the Fifth Section of the *Discours* Descartes offers two stated
reasons, and what in the end counts as a third reason, for a separation between humans and either animals or machines. This is the case
even though such machines (or animals) may resemble humans
and imitate their actions. (It should be noted that it is Descartes who
deploys the terms 'imitation' and 'resemblance'.) The first reason
pertains to language. For Descartes neither animals nor machines use
language. The specifically human activity is 'to declare to others our
thoughts' (1: 629) The second is that animals or machines only operate
in a determined way. Each organ has a disposition that causes it to
act in the way that it does. The comparison with human activity is
described by Descartes in the following terms.

> For, in the place of reason which is a universal instrument, that
> can serve in all sort of encounters, these organs have need of
> some particular disposition for each particular action. From which
> it follows that it is . . . impossible that there is enough diversity
> in a machine in order to make it act in all occurrences of life in
> the same way that our reason makes us act.
>
> (1: 629)

The third reason is that present in the human is an element that is
not comprised of 'matter', and which does not derive its power from
it and moreover will not die with the body. This is the *'l'ame
raisonnable'* (1: 631). What this means is that the mimetic economy
that is opened up by Descartes is limited by the conception of machine
and the introduction of the non-material. (Central here will be how
this non-material soul is to be understood.)

The problem now is to try and find a way of linking the exclusion
of the domestic and the failure to think placed activity, to the concern
that Descartes has with establishing self-certainty – where the latter is
interconnected, necessarily, to holding the human apart from any reduction to either animal or machine. What this means is that the mimetic
economy originally established must be effectively distanced. The *'l'ame
raisonable'* as non-material must be linked to the non-inclusion of the
domestic and the everyday.

Fundamental to the Cartesian project is the attempt to differentiate the operation of the body for those which related only to the '*l'ame raisonable*'. The soul, and this is true equally with the understanding and the role of thinking, as construed by Descartes, is that it brings with it an envisaged unity of the subject. On the level of the soul or thought, the subject can be, and moreover has to be, self-identical. It is precisely this set up that is captured in Descartes' famous formulation that 'I think therefore I am'. The 'I' as that which thinks is indistinguishable from the activity of thinking; and thus in the formulation '*cogito ergo sum*' the self (the ego) affirms itself as being, being itself, in the process of its thinking. To the question, what is the subject? – who is the Cartesian self? – the answer has to be that which thinks. Here the self is identified with the 'I'; with the ego. What is being staged in this opening therefore is a conception of the philosophical subject which, even though it may emerge in an act of differentiation, and, even if it may hold itself in position by the continuity of that differentiation, is, nonetheless, given as complete and thus having a self-completing finality. These two moments bring ontology – the existence of the subject – and temporality into conjunction. The latter, temporality, is given by the posited finality of self-completion. In the second place there is another possibility for thinking the self and thus for thinking its subjectivity.

Part of the difficulty with this position, however, is that while the Cartesian self was self-identical to the exclusion of its body, it could not eliminate the body. The body endured as an ineliminable remainder and therefore a constant reminder insofar as the body – operating as it does in terms feeling, pleasure, resemblance, etc. – remains as the continual source of error and deception. Having to maintain the body means that the Cartesian self is continually menaced by the possibility of deception and sin. It should not be forgotten that central to the project of the *Discours* is tying these two possibilities together. The pursuit of truth should not lead in any direction other than epistemological certainty and moral rectitude. And yet the body endures. Moreover it endures as the unmasterable element in the philosophical home. Here the body cannot be at home with philosophy even though it has to be with the thinking subject. The body has an ambivalent status that turns the home into a site of surveillance; a site in which the wants of the body – bodily wants not wanted by philosophy – have to be kept at bay by the watchful eye of the self-certain subject.

The house therefore is threatened by the presence of that which it cannot expel.

A consequence of this recognition of the place of the body – its inevitability – is that certain regimes, be they architectural or philosophical, are necessary in order to police the body. In other words, from what looks as thought it were no more than a philosophical argument concerning the centrality and envisaged unity of the self the fact that it is predicated on eliminating the body, a project that can only ever be partially successful and thus with the body returning as the unruly element in what would other wise a stable home, there emerges the necessity for a regime of control and thus the necessity for an organizational policy. The importance of this recognition is not the addition of this policy – in sum a form of politics – but that it has to have been there from the very start. The interarticulation of place and self – the interplay of shelter and the sheltered – was already the site that necessitated the imposition of mechanisms of control. Part of the way such controls work will be in the organization of space.

It is not difficult to link what has been identified thus far as a metaphysics of destruction to the attempted elimination of the body. Of the many ways in which this topic can be approached two of the most relevant concern, in the first place, the interconnection between memory and the body; in the second the relationship between the withdrawal of the domestic and the work of the soul. Memory and the body work in similar ways. The project of destruction encounters that which marks the impossibility of that project once the insistent presence of memory is recognized. Memory, in this precise sense, can be neither controlled nor policed with any absolute certainty by the work of destruction. It is present in the same way as the body remains an ineliminable element in the attempt to establish self-certainty. However, what is significant is that in the bodies's retention the body has to be controlled. In other words, as memory would have to be mastered the body will have to be managed in such a way that it was as though it had been eliminated. In both instances therefore there are versions of a metaphysics of destruction and attempts at mastery. As the body returns within an insistent presence that demands that consideration be given not just to its specificity – the specific presence of the body and thus of bodily differences – but with equal importance to the housing of that body. After all, the body is that which is sheltered. Once it has to be allowed a place then the question that inevitably arises is what is the place for this body. There is, of course, a similar move that has to be made in relation to memory. Since with memory there is the necessity to think through the complex repetitions – and they are repetitions that pertain as much to housing and the architectural as they do to the philosophical – and that which allows the work and the presence of memory a place.

What is intended to control the body is located outside the body. Outside but inside, the rational soul has to legislate for, and over, the body. The site of philosophical activity, the place of the self-certain subject attempts to exercise control over the body. However, control is also the impossibility of absolute control. Not only will the body remain the source of error, it necessitates the hold of that which legislates but which falls outside the realm of philosophy. At this point a connection emerges with the domestic. As has already been indicated the domestic while essential for the promulgation of the need for a philosophical revolution – articulated textually in terms of an architectural or urban destruction – was itself withdrawn from the necessity to which it gave rise. The domestic held back from the inception of complete change was merely to be subject to the unchanging repetition of law and custom. And yet the domestic has a fundamental ubiquity. It has to be managed and controlled otherwise it would upset the revolution that had been put in place, for Descartes, on the level of the philosophical. Apart from the possibility that such a conception of change locates it everywhere and yet nowhere, what it also entails is that to the extent that the domestic is held out of consideration – not positioned as a locus of radical change – it also has to be policed. The policing of the domestic is fundamental both to maintain the possibility of the successful enactment of a metaphysics of destruction and because, as with the body, it is the domain which while not falling under the sway of philosophy's rule has to be ruled. This latter point – the necessity of its having to be ruled – means that the domestic again as with the body, is the site the harbours the greatest potential precisely because it is the greatest threat.

Once it could be allowed that the body and the domestic fell within the domain of radical change, then to the extent that a metaphysics of destruction necessitates their exclusion, what would have to emerge is radical change as a consequence of their inclusion. Were this to be a possibility then architecture becomes a central concern. Where, given the ubiquity of the domestic and the complexity of bodies, would such

9

INTERRUPTING CONFESSION, RESISTING ABSOLUTION

MONUMENTS AFTER THE HOLOCAUST

OPENING ALTERITY

Otherness, its reality as well as its presence as a question, is inevitably at work within the Jewish question.[1] Prior however to any argument that stems from the acceptance of this point of departure, consideration needs to be given to otherness. Here, it is necessary to utilize a distinction. A distinction, no matter how initially tenuous – and, as with all distinctions subject to its own analysis – can still be drawn between the identity of being a Jew and Jewish being. The first element refers to the conception of the Jew at work within history of anti-semitism; in other words Christian thought's representation of the Jew. The second pertains to the conflict within Judaism concerning the question of Jewish identity.[2] The presence of anti-semitism is negotiated differently from within a concern for Jewish being – a Jewish response to the threat of assimilation or annihilation – than it would from within a more generalized concern for humanity. (While humanism may accept alterity the price of that acceptance may be alterity itself.) Despite a number of important differences between them, these two modalities of identity may none the less overlap. One point where this could occur would be in the struggle to differentiate them. Holding Jewish being apart from the conception of the Jew given within the history of anti-semitism may in fact have to recognize that any concern with Jewish being has to incorporate that history as a part of its own attempt to take up the question of identity.[3] In general terms, there are significant moments of imbrication at which the points of intersection and overlap work to define the possibility of important innovations in each domain; development as separate and combined.

The importance of the distinction redefines sites of activity. Pascal argues in the *Penseés*, drawing on a tradition that may still be at work within Christian thought, that the 'blindness' of the Jew is the foundation of Christianity itself. However, the response to such a claim cannot just involve the assertion of the contrary, namely that Jew's are in fact not blind. Pascal's claim operates simply on the level of the ascription of identity. It would be possible to generate a great many examples of this type. All would involve either a negative or pejorative description of Jewish identity. To offer a counter as a response – a move within a generalized structure of negation – would be to remain trapped within a self-determining either/or. Identity has to be posed otherwise. Hence the distinction, but also the nature of the distinction, between the identity of being a Jew and Jewish being.

The point that needs to be made is that the charge of blindness and the counter claim of sight would fail to address central questions of identity once they were posed within a preoccupation with Jewish being. It should be emphasized that what characterizes this conception of Being is conflict. Refusing the possibility of the essential and the unitary, redefines identity in terms of the presence of an inelim- inable conflict concerning identity. (Identity becomes identity in conflict.) It is also important to note here that the conception of naming compatible with this reformulation of identity has to take conflict as central. What the name identifies is at once pragmatic – there has to be a *there is* . . . – and yet that presence also signals the impossibility of the essential by the related affirmation of the primordial presence of conflict. This conception of the naming – conflict naming – is at its most dramatic when the name in question concerns the nation, or gender or racial identity.

In opposition to conflict naming there is a conception of naming that attempts to unify and thus to name an essential element of the whole. (And yet, of course, this presence of this opposition provides further evidence of the ineliminability of conflict.) At this point, it is important to add that memorials usually work in terms of an activity that allows for the reconstruction of the whole and, therefore, while the memorial always has regional force it is, for the most part, enacted in the name of unity. (This position will be developed at a later stage in terms of the conception of naming at work in what will be described as the logic of confession and absolution.) While the detail of these points needs to be developed in a more sustained manner, their immediate consequence is that they complicate the site in which the memorial or memorial is to be located. What is frustrated is any easy answer to questions concerning the subject positioning proper to the Holocaust memorial or memorial. The questions – for whom? on whose behalf? – become more exacting in the absence, though also with the retention, of a generalized humanity. Humanity remains a part of, though also as apart from, the centrality of Jewish being.

TOWARDS SPACING AND DISTANCING

Even operating within the province of the architectural or the urban, thinking alterity must allow the question of the other to endure as a question and thus for that questioning to be sustained as a task. What this means here is that alterity must always be linked to the specific; the particular generic repetition. Alterity becomes the other possibility for the museum, for the memorial, for the domestic house, etc. Alterity is defined in relation to that which is given and yet because of the centrality of conflict – identity as identity in conflict, conflict naming as the affirmed recognition of the impossibility of the essence – alterity does not have only one determination and thus one formal presence. Holding to the specificity of the object means that the task is delimited both by the presence of a formal and functional dominance within any genre and therefore by the varying forms possible within any generic repetition. (Alterity is defined in relation to the repetition of dominance.) What this entails is that this demanding conception of the task figure as that which orientates both the direction of action and the generation of the locus of judgement as they figure with the memorial or Holocaust memorial.[4] It is by maintaining a certain conception of particularity – recognizing that function and form are necessarily interarticulated – that it becomes possible to open up that which inheres within the more general problematic.

Moving to the general – a general of which the particular is not the instance but that which is given by recourse to moments of generic specificity, e.g. the museum, the hospital – what is at work here is the claim that, rather than the simple positing of the other, as though the position of the self (or the same) had already been secured either prior to, or in its differentiation from that other, a different route needs to be taken. Alterity needs to be understood as involved in a more complex sense of production. Alterity has to be removed from a logic of positing and thus withdrawn from its inscription within, and therefore from its dependence on a strict logic of oppositions. Part of such an undertaking is to define alterity in relation to repetition. Rather than destruction – negation as the source of alterity – repetition repositions the possibility as well as the formal presence of alterity in terms of distancing and spacing.

Distancing rids alterity of its utopian garb, since, rather than a complete opposition alterity necessitates that relation, albeit a relation of distance, forms an integral part of the work of alterity. The repositioning of spacing also involves relation. In this instance spacing introduces time. Spacing, moreover, has to be understood as inelimtably linked to the presence of the architectural. It has already been indicated that alterity always has to be defined in relation to the specific; here the architectural and within it the memorial. What this means is that spacing become a component of the object's work. Spacing is introduced into the interconnection between form and function such that form and function are held apart. Spacing allows for the transformation of function because it introduces an opening in which the incomplete is operative. The function in being realized, realized within its own transformation, holds open the particular function's precise determination, deferring its final realization by denying that function a formal finality.

The incomplete therefore marks the sustained presence of a function present in its being transformed. What this means is that the incomplete has the general result of resisting the closure that identifies alterity with a singular form. Specifically, in regards to the memorial, retaining the incomplete is to hold open the work of memory, insofar as the incomplete allows memory's work an opening and thus a form of continuity. (Emphasis, here, cannot be given to continuity *tout court*. The central issue is the *form* of continuity.) It is precisely the interplay of work and continuity held by maintaining the effective presence of the incomplete that can be defined as present remembrance. Remembrance, here, takes the present as central and thus the work's work is always be intended to sustain an opening thought in terms of vigilance. While the tradition of the memorial brings with it both incorporation and thus forgetting, vigilance formally present within the memorial structured by the formal work of present remembrance, works against an easy form of incorporation. Alterity is defined by, and therefore figures within this complex set up.

In sum, what this means is that alterity needs to be linked to distance in a more sustained and developed way. Distance, and with it a type of spacing, emerges as fundamental to a philosophical thinking of alterity, and thus figures within the concrete practice of memory at work within the process of establishing the memorial. Alterity's production demands the effective presence of distancing and spacing as themselves already implicated in the production of memory's work. Moreover, it is in terms of the latter – this specific form of memory's concrete practice – that it is possible to develop further what can be identified here as the task, now located within the a site delimited by the architectural and the urban, of present remembrance.

Two initial questions arise from this particular opening. They work to define the specificity of the Holocaust memorial. What, within that context, is meant by distance? How does the work of spacing figure within the memorial or monument? Specificity is needed. Not only because it defines the possibility of alterity, but also because abstraction entails an essentializing both of practice and the activity of memorialization itself. Again it is vital to be precise. Consequently, even at this early stage, it is necessary to distinguish between the museum and the memorial. While they may have important points of overlap, and while it may be possible to argue that the museum may be linked to the process of moumentalization, this is a one way process. The museum and the memorial stage different experiences, demanding different subject positions, because they operate with different conceptions of temporality and construction. The museum is already engaged with the problem of the relationship between built time – the way time inheres in the building's structuration – and more generalized questions of historical time. While the memorial may also engage that relationship, the former involves an implicated presence within architecture while the latter – the memorial – may figure within the urban, it may abut the architectural, nonetheless its point of reference is the place opened up by the complex interconnection of commemoration and public space. In this regard, a concern with a Holocaust museum opens up a related though nonetheless importantly different series of questions, than would be the case with a Holocaust monument or memorial. The presence of this difference lies as much within the history of the museum, as it does with the role of the memorial or monument within the construction, be it explicit or implicit, of the urban fabric.

While the museum encloses, in addition to its content though giving that content its coherence, what is enclosed is built time. The museum can work in terms of historical continuity – historicism in the guise of chronology – or it can work in terms of singular detached occurrences, in fact there can be a range of different ways in which historical time figures within the museum. Historical time is constructed by the museum's formal presence. As an object the museum works in terms of its realization of the effective presence of built time. In other words, the operation of built time is not simply a curatorial decision, rather it is the operation of time within the building's structuration. Even though, within the framework that allows the museum – here taken as a building – to be considered architecturally, may position it within the urban context, the central work of the museum has to be understood in terms of its own specific way of enclosing. Again, what needs to be emphasized here is the necessity to maintain particularity.

The museum's act of enclosure is to be addressed in terms of programme. It is precisely the museum's programme that cannot be readily separated from the operation of built time, since the articulation of time within its structure works to regulate the museums activity; i.e. regulate its work as a museum. The museum necessarily figures within the interplay between the process of enclosing and its already present articulation within the urban; its being enclosed within the urban. Following the latter would trace the movement of the museum's unfolding and thus its enclosure within the urban fabric. It would be this movement of enclosing and being enclosed that would allow a fruitful contrast to be drawn between, for example, Semper's *Kunsthistorisches Museum* in Vienna, the *Ringstrasse* and the generation of the city of Vienna on the one hand, and Richard Roger's *Centre Pompidou* and its urban presence within the city of Paris, on the others.[5] The initial point of contrast would be the different ways the relationship between enclosing and enclosure worked in each instance. Tracing those differences would allow an architectural analysis of their difference as museums to be developed. Such an analysis would take as its point of departure their presence as museums. Generic particularity would function as the point of departure. The absence of an essence means that the site of the generic repetition – the locus of analysis and judgement – only admits the particular and thus a workful economy of difference. Generic repetition and the economy of difference constructs a field of analysis because they generate and sustain both the possibility and the actuality of particularity.

It should not be overlooked that it is possible to interpret moments within the city – even part's of the city's own history – as implicated in the movement towards monumentalization. It would be possible, for example, to interpret the work of Hausmann in Paris, or the *Ringstrasse* itself as monuments; or at the very least as linked to the process of monumentalization. Equally, it would be possible to attribute a certain monumentality to the overall plan of the modern city. Nonetheless memorials still need to be held apart from the work of museums as museums. That museums can also be interpreted as monuments or memorials indicates the extent to which absolute generic separation is impossible. Equally, it attests to the risk of interpreting museums as monuments rather than as architecture.

MEMORIALS

Memorials, both in the extended sense of the construal of a building as a memorial, and usually in the limited sense of the attempt to commemorate a specific event or person, have a specific role. The straightforward manner of expressing this positioning is to argue that the memorial works to create a historical continuity. Whether it is a continuous history of the nation, or merely a town or a city, the memorial or memorial always seeks to include. Rewriting history by giving a history to the excluded, even writing a history of those who have been marginalized, creates a unified history once these moments of recovery are inscribed within an undifferentiated (and undifferentiating) national or local history.

The difficulty with this direct explication of the move to the memorial is that the straightforward explanation does no more than describe the operation of dominance. The repetition of the dominant tradition needs to be identified as such. The process of naturalization that works within the move to construct memorials would need to be exposed in the more general move which showed that the recourse to the naturalization of time was the work of dominance. It would, in addition, link exposure to what can be understood, though perhaps only initially, as the anti-memorial. The incursion of dominance and the related incorporation of the temporality of historicism, could be demonstrated by the aesthetics and politics of the anti-memorial. Again, what emerges is the possibility of alterity. The possibility of the anti-memorial already harbours questions pertaining to alterity. How is the 'anti' to be understood? In what way is such a memorial other than a memorial? How is the departure from structures of dominance to be understood? These questions delimit the field of spacing and distancing. Fundamental to any answer that can be given to them is the complex interplay of dominance and the temporality of historicism since they work together defining the potential site of unity and with it of inclusion. Furthermore, taking up these questions cannot neglect particularity: Here the particularity of the Holocaust memorial.

Writing of Hans Haacke's *Und ihr habt doch gesiegt* Michael North argues that as a work it,

> manages to superimpose one public space on another and in so doing suggests a community whose nature is open to question, whose history presents certain alternatives for choice. A memorial like this does not represent the continuity of the present with the past but rather the chance, through an awakened public opinion, to break a dependence on the past reinforced by silence.[6]

Haacke's work is not a Holocaust memorial. None the less, its concern is to fracture conceptions of time that work in terms of continuity on the one hand and forgetting on the other. By repeating the presence of a Nazi memorial in the centre of Graz in 1988, the nature of the connection between its original construction in 1938 and the contemporary is dramatized. What was it that had been excised? What had been retained with the memorial? It was impossible to escape the hold of these emphatic and disturbing questions. Questions, rather than a forced didacticism, condition any experience of the work.

If this work is an anti-memorial its alterity is defined by the copresence of continuity and discontinuity. The alterity is not absolute. Hence the question of relation is central. The continuity is not absolute. Hence the question of the discontinuous is central. Both work together defining a site that resists mastery since the interplay of continuity and discontinuity, same and other, yield a site that retains the work of the incomplete. It retains it without loss since there had never been a prior state of completion. It is precisely the effective presence of the incomplete that generates another conception of the memorial's work. Indeed, it is for this reason that the term anti-memorial is in the end inappropriate. There is alterity within the project of monumentality. However the expression anti-memorial (or anti-monument) works to give the memorial a singular determination and thus it obscures the fact that what is actually at work is the operation of dominance. And yet, what the expression opens up is the obligation of having to think a version of the memorial's other – alterity within a reworked process of monumentalization – precisely because it leaves the nature of alterity, the work of the 'anti', unthought. As will emerge, once it comes to be thought, this is a thinking conditioned by the effective presence of distancing and spacing.

In a recent discussion of the role of memorials and monuments within the German context, Andreas Huyssen has argued that their intrusion into the urban fabric brings with it an attendant risk.

The more memorials there are, the more the past becomes invisible, the easier it is to forget: redemption, thus, through forgetting. Indeed, many critics describe Germany's current obsession with memorials and memorials as the not so subtle attempt at *Entsorgung*, the public disposal of radio-active historical waste.[7]

Huyssen's work plots the curious move from what he describes as an 'antifascist antimonumentalism' to the current obsession with the memorial within the now unified state of Germany.[8] While it is not difficult to incorporate this latter move into the process of unification – forgiveness, especially the self-forgiving move occurring as a type of public acknowledgement, the public avowal of a generalizing and thus unifying *mea culpa* that at the moment of being announced yields absolution and allows a return to the continuity of life – the difficulty, nonetheless, is identifying the countermove to this set up. In other words, the question that arises from Huyssen's argument concerns the possibility of another response; namely, a response recognizing the necessity for the process of memorialization but which is not trapped by the difficulties opened up because of the linkage between the construction of the memorial and the subsequent process of forgetting.

The temptation is to counter continuity with discontinuity; unification with another formulation of disunity. The difficulty emerges once these positions are understood as articulated within a defining either/or. The strategies arising from distancing and spacing, because they hold to the centrality of relation thus allowing for the copresence of continuity and discontinuity, unity and disunity (where all the elements would be transformed by their mutual copresence) works with (and within) the abeyance of this either/or. In this instance with the abeyance of the either/or there emerges the need to respond to another logic. Here because the either/or is defined by, though it also defines, the logic of confession and absolution, alterity is conditioned by that logic's work. What this means is that the site of engagement and thus the possibility of alterity does not involve countering continuity with discontinuity, or unity with disunity, but is situated in relation to the logic of confession and absolution. It is within the terms of developing a counter logic – the alterity positioned by the presence of confession and absolution- that the distinction between the identity of being a Jew and Jewish being has to be reintroduced.

The Holocaust memorial within the European context inevitably has a particular and thus a regional force. Particularity always needs to be retained. If it is possible to generalize then it would seem that such memorials or monuments become the public acknowledgement of a wrong. There is an inevitable problem that emerges here concerning language. Once it is possible to write of a 'wrong' then it would seem necessary to introduce a more precise terminology. In the place of wrong could it not be argued that what took place was 'evil'? As a beginning it should not be thought that there is an appropriate word. What has to be recognized is that these words stage a particular conception of human agency and historical time. Evil, especially Kant's conception of 'radical evil', position agency in terms of abstraction and unity. Evil allows the agent the possibility of an overcoming that enables a reabsorbing of that agent into the continuity of humanity. Linked to this structure is the work of a particular formulation of historical time. Within it time moves forward with the reacceptance into the whole of the now expunged evil or wrong. The movement through chronology becomes the move in which the disposition leading to evil is measured and then excised. In other words evil or wrong thus construed becomes articulated within conceptions of historical time and subjectivity in which the movement of chronology comes to be renamed as progress.

The movement of time, and in this instance it is no more than the movement of historical time, allows for the expression of culpability at the same time as it is the denial of the culpability of the present. Confession or acknowledgement concede the aberration and at the same time withdraw the present moment – the moment present within chronological time – from any implication into that which was aberrant. (The aberration was, it occurred, it has taken place and is no longer. What was is no more. What had been no longer pertains.) It should be noted, immediately, that the response to this set up is not to argue that the present generation is to blame and thus that they should feel guilt. This move merely repeats the logic of confession and absolution and invites the counter claim that would ask; when does the moment of absolution occur? At what point within the unfolding of chronological time will it be allowed? Name the moment of redemption! Though in whose name will it be named? The irony is, of course, that as the act of forgiveness is self-imposed – imposed, here, as a beginning, in the name of national unity – this question may be as sincere as it is otiose.

THE LOGIC OF CONFESSION AND ABSOLUTION

Confession and absolution demand the intrusion of the name. In fact the logic of confession both yields and demands a name; to confess is to name. Naming cannot be equated with the identification of sin. In such a case identification would be no more than the act of individuation allowing the sinner to be identified and the particular sins to be counted. Naming is the invocation of that name which recognizes the sin as a sin. Absolution can only be given in the name of that which deems the actions to have been sinful. Confession, therefore, generates a name as much as it necessitates a name. The logic of confession and absolution works to identify the place of sin – the sin occurred in your name against your name – and the possibility of absolution as the reasserting of the name. The latter is, of course, a reassertion freed from the present mark of the past. Once again it is a freedom that is merely putative.

This set up has the consequence that the site in which the sin is acknowledged has an amoral quality, or at the very least it is projected as such. Riding the site of a moral quality – locating questions of

morality within the movement from confession to absolution – enables
the site, within the work of this logic, to function as a place of recall.
What is recalled is the sin now absolved. The present site is itself
absolved from any participation in that which countered as the sin.[9]
Indeed, such would be the condition of possibility for a memorial that
took place within the logic of confession and absolution and which
occurred within – and for – the name; the name of national unity.
Linking the memorial or the Holocaust memorial to national unity is
to locate its work within this logic. Two fundamental points take place
with this identification. Both are interrelated insofar as both refer to
time. In the first instance sin and absolution create a conception of
unity that yields an occurrence that in being identified as aberrant may
then, and only then, come to be excised. It is the identification and
the act of excision that creates the unity. The second is the possible
pathology inherent in the logic of confession; a pathology emerging
because of the impossibility of either a sustained active forgetting or
a systematic disavowal.

   What is at work in the first of these points emerges from the contrast
between two differing conceptions of the relationship between action
and time. In the first instance, the temporality of the memorial can
be understood as the singular moment that in asserting its singularity
in the name of the whole allows for its reabsorbtion back into the
whole. (The singular, even the aberrant singular, was already part of
the whole.) Here, time is construed in terms of continuity. The aberrant is able to appear as part of the whole once acknowledged and
then deemed as aberrant it reappears as devalued. It is, of course,
precisely as an intervention against the possibility of this devaluing,
or perhaps more accurately to show its impossibility, that Hans Haake's
already cited work can be understood. The second conception redefines the relationship between action and time. This redefinition does
not take place in terms set by the negation of continuity. On the
contrary, it emerges from the affirmed centrality of what can be
described as an interrupted continuity. Interruption and continuity –
always understood as copresent in their difference – signal the
primordality of relation. It with this second possibility that not only
does another temporal determination open up, what takes place necessitates the abeyance of the possibility of a complete and final absolution
because of the inscription of an ineliminable spacing. The impossibility
of completion yields strategies that involve distance. Spacing and

distancing mark the presence of relation. Moreover, they mark the projected impossibility of absorption.

What this means is that because the logic of confession and absolution demands the effacing of relation and thus the elimination of a primordial spacing countering this logic demands recourse to the affirmation of that spacing. Rather than a simple negation affirmation here means the affirmation of relation and with it the recognition of the ineliminability of the interplay of continuity and discontinuity, and unity and disunity. It is this latter point – the countermove – that needs to be developed.

The assertion of unity that occurs with the name's work is necessarily mythic in the precise sense that in eliminating that which would tear the whole – or rather that which have already torn it – it is this deliberative act that allows for the reasserting of the whole. What makes this mythic is not the recourse to an origin – even though such a move may in fact take place – but the fact that the space between assertion and reassertion is a non-space. To reassert after the event is the attempt to excise the event; as such there is only the assertion of unity and identity. (It is essential to add that what is at work here is not the excision in and of itself but the attempt to excise. Allowing it to be an attempt whose failure is possible, is to acknowledge the possible pathology within the logic of confession.) With the realization of this attempt – and in terms of its having a singular effect – the discontinuous would have been incorporated by its having been acknowledged. The attempted incorporation of the discontinuous involves two fundamental elements. The first is that it must position the singular as part of the whole; the aberrant part. The second is that there is the working assumption that the incorporation can be both possible and successful. Both parts figure within the construction of a memorial enacted within the interplay of the logic of confession and absolution on the one hand and the mythic on the other. Both work to eliminate the spacing between the assertion and the subsequent reassertion of unity. It is in these terms that forgetting is realized.

If there is any viability to the description of the mythic in this context as predicated up the elimination of space – the spacing between the asserting and the reasserting – then it provides, in addition, a locus for the process of demythologization. Rather than presenting a counter myth, demythologization works within that envisaged non-space by providing it with the presence of an ineliminable spacing. What this means is that not only is there the deliberate yielding of space, it is also the case that such a move reveals the always possible primordial spacing that would have been at work within the gap between asserting and reasserting. Its already present existence denied by the work of the logic and confession and reabsorbtion would, none the less, continue to make itself present in terms of symptoms. Given this possibility what, then, does it mean to affirm the presence of an already present spacing?

SPACING, THE INCOMPLETE: SITES OF JUDGEMENT

Spacing insists. The difficulty, however, is to account for that possibility – the insistent presence of spacing – within the activity of memory and thus within the concrete practice of memorialization. What occurs when spacing can be said to insist within this practice and thus when it plays a determining role within the monument? Perhaps, it is best to begin with what appears to be the more intractable problem. It has already been suggested that not only is the intrusion of spacing an architectural possibility but that there is also a sense in which a primordial spacing is at work within architecture despite the attempt, by that architecture, to eliminate its presence and thus its work. The architecture in question is the architecture of tradition.[10] Two questions arise here. What is this primordality? Moreover, what is a primordial spacing within this architecture?

Architecture is determined by the formula that form follows function. However, this formulation loses its monolithic quality once it is recognized that function does not have a direct formal expression since it is already the site of potential or actual conflict. That this always appears to be resolved in only one direction does no more than evidence the way dominant traditions work within architecture. The function and nature of the domestic, for example, remains untouched because its site of repetition – the domestic house – is for the most part the same. It is articulated within the logic of the Same. Again, it is essential to be precise. The logic of the Same does not entail that each house is identical, or that they appear identical. Rather, each house is the same insofar as the architecture of any one house allows for the repetition of the already existent structure of the domestic. Interventions – to the extent that interventions are possible – can only occur within these repetitions. If there is an architectural critique of the domestic and its related patriarchal structure then the locus of intervention – the site of judgement – is within the work of specific repetitions. Consequently, it is within this structure that the question of the primordial needs to be posed.

Within the reciprocity of form follows function, if there is a repetition of dominance how could there also be, in addition, any form of primordial presence? The answer is already present in the question. Primordial presence is, of course, this addition. In other words, what primordial presence means in this instance is a way of accounting for a consequence or an affect that is not reducible to a constituent part of the concrete presence of the form/function relation. What is primordially present could be the inscription of a desire for completion. It could be the attempt to close the question of function by giving it an exact form. There are other ways of formulating instances of that which is primordially present. Their defining characteristics, however, are always linked to the registration of a particular intention or desire. It should not thought that simply because there is an inscription of a certain desire that the desired effect has not been realized. It is at this point that there is an important difference between the operation of literary or philosophical texts on the one hand, and architecture on the other. While the project of completion within the literary or the philosophical may be subject to an analysis that demonstrates the impossibility of that project – namely an analysis that would trace the foundering of any attempt to establish an object marked by a self-completing finality – architecture resists this possibility. It resists it for at least two reasons. In the first instance because of what is involved in the experience of architecture. And in the second because of the practices within which architecture takes place. Completion and finality are more than mere possibilities within architecture.

The inscribed desire for completion or even the attempt to produce a minimal space apparently devoid of programmatic and functional considerations, always has the determinations proper to the function in question at work within it. The presence of any function already entails the different subject positionings demanded by the successful reproduction of that function. What this means is that the possibility of completion always has present within it other structural possibilities and thus other subject positions. In other words, within the setting itself there is the potential for the actualization of the tensions that the successful reproduction of dominant functions has to preclude. The potential for conflict, and thus the pathology occurring with its repression are ineliminable elements within the reproduction of dominance. There is therefore a fragility within the setting that the determination of function demands and that the architecture in question works to hold in place. The form/function relation is therefore overdetermined. What marks out the presence of this overdetermination, and hence the fragility, is the tension within the function sustained by the specific architectural occurrence. This overdetermination is at work within the function – the tensions generated by it may be, in fact, exasperated by the specific formal presence of the architecture in question – and yet it is not reducible to the concrete presence of the architecture. The overdetermined presence of function is primordially present. What this introduces into the work of architecture – even into those works that envisage a strong relationship between form and function – is a complexity that insists from the moment of the work's inception.

It is in terms of the identification of the presence of this inherent complexity that it becomes necessary to distinguish between function's traditional expression, bringing with it an overdetermination that exposes the inherently unstable nature of the exercise of that function, and what has already been identified as the incomplete. In the first instance there is the inherent pathology within completion; in the second there is the possibility of an affirmation of the incomplete. It needs to be underlined that the second position – the incomplete – is not a negation of the former – the complete. The 'in' of the incomplete marks a distancing not a negation. This occurs in the precise sense that what is held in place is a function present in its being transformed. (Transformation, while taking place, indeed it is the work of architecture, is located beyond the hold of a straightforward teleological development. Transformation, in the sense suggested here, demands the abeyance of a predetermined telos.) The 'in' of the incomplete sustains the function – relation is an ineliminable part of distancing – and yet the precise determinations of that function are not given formally despite function having a necessary and therefore inescapable presence. This resistance of finality is the work of the inscribed presence of spacing.

Spacing, as that which resists finality, is inextricably linked to distancing. With the distancing of a particular functional determination, the functional is still retained. Spacing as that which occasions distancing, occasioning by being copresent with it, can only ever be considered in relation to its operation within a specific architectural economy, and, therefore any consideration of spacing depends upon the particularity of the function being considered. Spacing while generating form cannot be approached as though it did not bear a direct relation to questions of function and programme. In this instance, what is of concern is the way in which the presence of a memorial or a monument that works in terms of a reabsorbing into a whole, and thus a concern with memorialization that takes place in the name of unity, is inappropriate to any thinking of a Holocaust memorial.

There are two reasons why this is the case. The first is that the relationship between absorption and forgetting entails that such a conception of memorialization would bring with it the conditions for forgetting the Holocaust rather than for remembering it. The task of memory vanishes once the 'aberrant' has been identified and then absorbed. The second is that the distinction between the identity of being a Jew and Jewish being must complicate the question of remembrance insofar as it complicates the subject positioning proper to memory's concrete work. The problem of the name and thus the type of unity that naming brings with it take on a different form once any response to the question of identity has to concede the presence of a founding complexity and thus the insistence of anoriginal difference. To remember for the sake of the all, remembering in order to hold onto to, or to create unity, even that curious conception of unity generated by the operation of the logic of confession and absolution, are conceptions of unity and totality that will have been rendered impossible to the extent that the division within Jewish identity is accepted. (In other words, the impossibility arises as soon as identity is linked to a question rather than finality.) These two reasons need to be developed. In developing them it is possible to clarify why the effective presence of spacing is a necessity within the Holocaust memorial. It should not be thought that its presence can only have one form. The fact that there is not a formal equivalent indicates why here there has to be a connection between architectural or artistic invention and the concrete work of memory. In regards to the work of memory – perhaps for memory to have work and thus for the project of present remembrance to be at work – spacing is the *sine qua non*.

Perhaps the enduring result of the Holocaust is its endurance. As an occurrence it continues to work within the processes of creation;

it continues to haunt artistic production; it remains as a legacy defying philosophy. Its insistence gives it a pivotal position within any understanding of the operation of modernity. How is it possible to work in relation to its insistence? This is a question that is specific to any one attempt to create work. How is its insistence to be registered? This becomes the architectural question once it is reformulated in terms of asking for a memorialization for that which refuses the sleep that the inattentive attention of mere memory may enjoin. Even if it were successful such a move – memory yielding forgetting – always harbours its own possible interruption. The irruption marking repression's failure is the interruption of the continuity envisaged by, and for, the name of unity. Guarding against that moment generates the task of redescribing that which would have been aberrant in order then to be absorbed or incorporated. Resisting continuity is resisting the mythic; part of that resistance is the exposure of continuity as an imaginary construct dependant upon the myth of national unity.

  Working within the logic of confession and absolution the memorial is articulated within the need for incorporation. This is a move taking place in the name of unity. The identity of the people – the people as name and thus as named – has an essential singularity. The memorial both opens and is enclosed within the whole, in its name and for its name. Taken together naming and an essential singularity structure a memorial facilitating forgetting. Countering this set up does not just demand a memorial resisting absorption, it must achieve this end by complicating the process of naming. Naming must work otherwise. Again, starting with unity, a memorial that works in the name of unity generates a single subject position. It is only to the extent that identification with the name is possible that the memorial or monument can position the subject as addressed by it. Naming and the memorial (the memorial taking place in the name of unity) while appearing to work in terms of a generalized humanity usually identifies that generality with the specific nation and in so doing refuses the particularity of identity. What this means is that generality in actually referring to the nation understood as an undifferentiated totality cannot generate the subject position that is other than that of the envisaged unity. In this instance, what this entails is the preclusion of that conception of identity that is articulated in relation to sustaining the effective copresence – at time the overlapping copresence – of the identity of being and Jew and Jewish being.

Once it becomes possible to fracture the unity that is given with a mythic conception of the people then, with the shift in the subject positioning, a new relationship takes place. The important point here is that shift does not take place within the confines of an either/or. Rather, what emerges with this fracturing is an opening up of possible subject positions. By possible was is meant is a positioning that allows, for example, for the position that places the Jew as a constitutive part of a generalized humanity. (The corollary is that Jew is allowed to be a member of the people as thus to be named by the recitation of that nation's name; the naming having moved from its being structured by the essential to its involving the reiteration of conflict. Once again, it is this latter conception of naming that take place with(in) the abeyance of the essential.) This positioning is not all inclusive for at the same time – and it is vital in this instance to underline the importance of this temporal simultaneity – there is the necessary inclusion of a complicating twofold movement. The twofold presence of a set up that positions the Jew as *a part of* a generalized humanity – or national variant thereof – and *apart from* that conception of unity becomes the articulation of the imbrication of identity as given – the identity of being a Jew – and the conflict marking the attempts to establish identity. The latter is identity structured by the question, it is identity in conflict and therefore it is the conception of identity proper to what has been called thus far Jewish being. At work within it is an ineliminable spacing. One form of identity cannot be reduced to other. The possibility of formal innovation exists to the extent that spacing is sustained within the work.

Finally, therefore, it has already been suggested that operating merely on the level that only allows for a subject position working in terms of generalized humanity always runs the risk of the exclusion of alterity where alterity is thought within the confines of, for example, Jewish being. It allows for alterity but only if alterity is conceived as opposing the negative conception of the other that works within the tradition of identity as an ascription as coming from outside. The example that has already been given is to position the Jew as blind and responding with a negation of that claim by advancing the counter assertion that Jews are not blind. The attribution of sight would allow for the Jew to be included as the Jew would have become the Same. And yet, as has already been indicated, what this general set up also entails – and it entails it with a formal necessity – is the retention of a subject

ANNOTATED GUIDE
TO FURTHER READING

Over the last 20 years greater emphasis has been paid to the separate area of architectural theory than had hitherto. Architectural theory emerged as an important aspect of architectural writing and equally architectural pedagogy. Tracing the history of this movement or development has yet to be undertaken on the level of a concrete analysis. However four recent anthologies bring together extremely important work written by the leading contributors to the area. Two volumes edited by K. Michael Hayes, one by Neil Leach and another by Kate Nesbitt represent the range of possibilities within contemporary theory.[1] The two volumes edited by K. Michael Hayes – *Architecture/Theory/ Since 1968* and the *Oppositions Reader* – are of particular significance. The first volume is chronologically structured. Its value is that it allows the reader to trace the development of architectural theory as it unfolds through time. It becomes possible to integrate the developments within political theory and philosophy by articulating them along the same time line. This volume contains text by theorists as well as by contemporary architects – e.g. Eisenman, Leibeskind, Tschumi – who were and are actively immersed in the development of theoretical concerns. The volume gives a great deal of emphasis to American authors. In a sense this is correct as the major developments with architectural theory have emerged from America. Central to the development of theory was the Institute for Architecture and Urban Studies. The Institute published the journal *Oppositions*. It was edited by Peter Eisenman, Kurt Forster, Kenneth Frampton, Mario Gandelsonas and Anthony Vidler. All still major figures in the domain of architectural theory and history in addition to some also being practising architects. The *Oppositions Reader* presents the major texts from a journal whose existence in the late 1970s and early 1980s allowed for the development of theory as a separate though nonetheless integral site of activity within architectural schools.

The volumes edited by Nesbitt and Leach complement these volumes. Nesbitt's volume presents theoretical work from 1965–95. Rather than allowing chronology to set the stage she pursues the history of theory during that period in terms of topics. Particularly valuable in her collection are the text grouped under the heading 'Urban Theory and Modernism' and 'The School of Venice'. The texts by Rowe, Koetter, Hoolhaus, Rossi and Tafuri open up domains often closed off within discussion of theory. Leach's Anthology is more European in orientation and more concerned with texts by cultural historians and philosophers. All the leading figures, from Derrida and Jameson to Eisenman and Tschumi are presented in these volumes. Taken together they would provide the basis for any introduction to this broad yet demanding topic of study.

Perhaps the most important shift that has occurred with architectural theory is – to use a generalized formulation – the move from a concern with meaning to a concern with form. A new generation of architects and theorists – some occupying both positions – has emerged with this development. While compiling a list of names – individuals and offices – is always invidious amongst those central to this move area Greg Lynn, Jeffrey Kipnis, Reiser and Umemoto, Ben Van Berkel, Bernard Cache, Foreign Office, Sanford Kwinter, Catherine Ingraham, Robert Somol, Elizabeth Grosz and Stan Allen. As yet there is not an extensive bibliography of book and articles. Nonetheless, there are some important publications. Greg Lynn has recently published *Animate Form*, Princeton University Press, New York, 1999 and *Folds, Bodies and Blobs: Collected Essays*, La lettre volée, Brussels, 1998. These books are fundamental to an understanding of the way the production of form is now central to the activity of architecture – a centrality that is allowing the computer to play a greater role in architectural practice than ever before. It is a role that is still to be given an adequate theoretical account. Bernard Cache has written *Earth Moves: The Furniture of Territories*, trans. Ann Boyman, MIT Press, Cambridge, 1995. Cache's work has opened and contributed to important developments in topology. The yearly volume produced from the ANY conferences and edited by Cynthia Davidson is an important collection that in its own way is detailing part of the history of the move to form. The volumes are now published in conjunction with

MIT Press. Another source for work in the area is the journal *Assemblage*. Other works that play an important role in the development of a new conception of form and the thus another thinking of geometry include Catherine Ingraham *Architecture and the Burden of Lineararity*, Yale University Press, New Haven, 1998; and Stan Allen, *Practice. Architecture, Technique and Representation*. G&B Arts, The Netherlands, 2000.

One of the topics that has emerged from a concern with form is the diagram. In part this interest has developed from an engagement with Deleuze's work on the diagram as it occurs both in his study of Foucault and in his work on Bacon.[2] Of the many texts to appear on the diagram two of the most important are Ben Van Berkel: The Proto-Functional Potential of the Diagram in Architectural Design, in *El Croquis* 72/73, 1995, and Peter Eisenman, *Diagram Diaries*. Thames and Hudson, London, 1999. (The latter also contains an exceptional text by Robert Somol 'Dummy Text or the Diagrammatic Basis of Contemporary Architecture.')

What marks out the majority of this work is a twofold process. On the one hand there is a return to a consideration of the object as an architectural object. On the other, central to that return, is a consideration of form not as a static entity but as that which is produced. It should not be though that there is a simple position being propounded within these works. Indeed there are dramatic and important differences. Nonetheless what remains as central is the object's self-realization as architecture.

NOTES

PREFACE

1 If it were not for the kindness and intellectual generosity of Bernard Tschumi at Columbia and Mohsen Mostafavi and Mark Cousins at the Architectural Association I would not have had the opportunity to undertake the research and teach the courses the lead to the writing of this book. In many ways this book is the tale of two institutions.

2 While earlier versions of these texts exist, all have been rewritten, some extensively, for this present volume. Original places of publication are as follows:
Chapter 1 Unpublished.
Chapter 2 *Korean Journal of Architecture*, No. 19, 1997.
Chapter 3 in *Reiser and Umemoto. Recent Work*, Academy Editions, 1998.
Chapter 4 *Journal of Philosophy and the Visual Arts*, No. 3, 1992.
Chapter 5 *AA Files*, No. 37, 1997.
Chapter 6 *ANY*, No. 23, 1998.
Chapter 7 *Architectural Design*, No 64, November/December, 1993.
Chapter 8 In Neil Leach (ed.) *Architecture after the Revolution*, Routledge, London, 1998.
Chapter 9 Unpublished.

INTRODUCTION

1 The term 'object' is used here to designate a particular architectural event. While particularity is important and thus the differences between diagrams, plans and buildings need to be maintained, it is also possible to generalize. It is this generalization that is identified by use of the term 'object'.

CHAPTER 1

1 Peter Eisenman. Blurred Zones: The Time of the Vertical Plane. Lecture given at AIT Berlin.

2 The texts in questions are Plato *Timaeus*, Loeb Classical Library, Harvard University Press, Cambridge, 1952. J. Derrida 'Khora' in *On the Name*, translated by Ian McLeod, Stanford University Press, 1995 (original French edition

Khora Editions Galilée, Paris 1993) and G. Bataille, 'L'informe' in *Oeuvres Completes*, Tome. 1, Gallimard, Paris, 1970, p. 217. All future references will be to these editions. The reference will be given as sections number in the case of Plato and page number in the case of Derrida and Bataille.

3 Maintaining the futural possibility of the yet-to-be as a quality of the present allows, on the one hand for the capacity for innovation and experimentation to be a quality of the present and not the consequence of simple speculation. On the other hand it precludes the possibility of prescription precisely because the future is contained as that which awaits precise programmatic possibility within a setting which is itself already at work. The important consequence is that an architecture that allows for a futural possibility cannot itself determine – architecturally – the form that the future will take. There need to be a formulae that will capture this possibility. It can be developed in terms of two importantly different senses of addition or relation. The first is additive while the second involves temporal complexity. In regards to the first: it is conceivable that a particular building may have two different organizational logics (e.g. individual floor slabs on the one hand and a spiral elevation on the other), or that a given building take on an addition such that the addition has no further consequence than the addition itself. Both instances can be formulated in the following terms – $x + y = x + y$. What this means is that either the copresence of x and y or the addition of y to x has no further consequences than either simple copresence or addition. The equal sign is a neutral space. There is however another positioning. Within it addition moves from the domain of the additive to one sustained by the yet-to-be determined and thus by an insistent complexity. Here $x + y = x + y + z$. The z can be seen as the unpredictable consequence of the interarticulation of x and y, or the consequence of their addition. The move across the equal sign has to be marked by the necessary absence of a final determination and thus prediction. Production eschewing the formal presence of prediction gives rise to what can be called the z factor. The z factor can have both programmatic consequences or be the result of formal manipulations with programmatic effects. The details of these possibilities are presented in Chapters 2 and 3. At this stage what needs to be noted is that it is a way of inscribing a yet-to-be determined quality into the building's realization as a building.

4 There is an important theoretical and practical point that needs to be made here. One of the significant consequences of holding to a rigorous distinction between architecture and either conceptual art of sculpture is that it then allows the question of their relation to be posed. Moreover, it can be posed in such a way that the margins can come to define the particularity of the architectural. The limit would delimit the centre. If there is a conflation of these separate domains undertaken on the basis of subject matter then a simplistic conception of content would come to define activity. Criticality would vanish because the loss of generic specificity means that what is in fact lost is the site of critical intervention.

5 The most important work here is by Rosalind Krauss and Yves Alain-Bois. While the term and its effects have been deployed within their writings at

different times they have produced a joint work that provides a more sustained version. See their *Formless*, MIT Press, Boston, 1997. For a different, and in the end, more persuasive use of this term see Georges Didi-Huberman, *La ressemblance informe*, Macula, Paris, 1995.

6   Two of most important philosophical studies of the *Timaeus* are Luc Brisson *Le meme et l'autre dans la structure ontologique du Timée de Platon*. Editions Klincksieck. Paris. 1874. (Brisson translates khora as 'milieu spatial') and John Sallis *Chorology*, Indiana University Press, Bloomington, 1999. Derrida and Eisenman have also been involved on a joint project related to the text, see their *Choralworks*, Monacelli Press, New York, 1998. Part of the argument presented here can be read as a response to elements of that project.

7   What emerges here is what can be defined as the logic of khora. This logic states the following; whatever it is that is deployed or used to establish a given x cannot either have or assume any of the determining qualities of x. In regards to law the claim has to be that the origin of law – where origin is understood as that which establishes law's law like qualities – cannot itself have any of these qualities or even the form of law. While formulations such as these avoid the circular tautology in which the cause has to have the same quality as the effect, it none the less gives rise to a number of different philosophical problem. In this context that is not the issue. The important point is that this logic is used by Derrida and others in their engagement with the text. While it works as an important philosophical device, what is not clear is its architectural utility.

8   Bataille references will be to the Oeuvres Complètes (OC) volume number followed by page number.

9   All these texts can be found in OC, 1.

10 The entire text is as follows:

> Un dictionnaire commencerait à partir du moment où il ne donnerait plus les sens mais les besognes des mots. Ainsi *informe* n'est pas seulement un adjectif ayant tel sens mais un chose servant à déclasse, exigeant généralement que chaque chose ait sa forme. Ce qu'il désigne n'a ses droits dans aucun sens et se fait écraser partout comme une araignée ou un ver de terre. Il faudrait en effet, pour que les hommes académiques soient contents, que l'univers prenne forme. La philosophie entière n'a pas d'autre but: il s'agit de donner une redingote à ce qui est, une redingote mathématique. Par contre affirmer que l'univers ne ressemble à rien et n'est qu'*informe* revient à dire que l'univers est quelque chose comme une araignée ou un crachat.

The project of the next section of this chapter is to work through this text. Rather than proceed from beginning to end, this short entry needs to be understood as a site occasioning different – often strategically different – returns. In each instance a translation of the relevant lines will be given. Precisely because the complexity of translation is an integral part of any treatment and thus interpretation of this 'entry' no attempt will be made to give a translation in advance.

11 It is in tracing this event in Bataille's own engagement with explicitly onto-logical concerns – in this instance in 'Le labyrinthe (ou la composition des êtres)' in *L'expérience intérieure* (OC, V: 97–115)) – that it would be possible to identify the work of the plural event within Bataille's engagement at the limit of philosophy.

12 This section of this chapter can be read therefore as continuing my engage-ment with the architecture of Peter Eisenman. The other papers I have written on Eisenman include:

Peter Eisenman and the Housing of Tradition, *Oxford Art Journal*, 1989. A rewritten version was printed in my *Art, Mimesis and the Avant-Garde*, Routledge, London, 1991.

Re:working Eisenman: Work and Name, in *RE:WORKING EISENMAN*, St, Martins Press, New York, 1993.

Architecture et Contrainte, *Chimères*, No. 17, pp. 139–54, 1993.

Resisting Ambivalence: Form and Function in Eisenman's Architecture. Originally published in *Korean Journal of Architecture*, No. 14, 1997. A modified version is published here as Chapter 2.

13 Peter Eisenman. Zones of Undecidability: The Process of the Interstitial, in Cynthia Davidson (ed.) *Anyhow*, MIT Press, Boston, 1998, pp. 31–2.

14 Eisenman, ibid. p. 32.

15 This opening in which the present possibility of the future comes to de defined as internal to the operation of the building has to be given a specific descrip-tion. This will be pursued here is in terms of the logic of the a part/apart. (This logic will be developed in this chapter as well as in subsequent ones.) The point of this formulation is twofold. In the first instance it acknowledges the primordality of function. The *a part of* and the *apart from* are defined by the differing possibilities for the repetition of tradition. The second is that it will allow for developing further the way in which an object – here a building – can be positioned as a complex site. Complexity means anoriginal irreducibility. The presence of this logic as at work *ab initio* affirms such a conception of complexity.

16 Eisenman, Blurred Zones: The Time of the Vertical Plane.

17 A more detailed discussion of this project is given in the final part of Chapter 2.

CHAPTER 2

1 The range of writing on Eisenman's work is vast. There are specific books and articles linked to specific projects. A diverse range of philosophers and architects have engaged with his work. A detailed bibliography is available in the forthcoming *Eisenmanual* from Monacelli Press, New York, 2000. It would involve a different type of text to this one to engage with the range

of positions. The history of the reception of Eisenman's work is integral to the significant movements within architectural theory. The contrast between, for example, the following articles by Michael Hays and Robert Somol – articles separated by only nines years – would be productive because it opens the site in which architectural theory has developed. See K. Michael Hays, From Structure to Site to Text in K. Michael Hays and Carol Burns (eds) *Thinking the Present. Recent American Architecture*, Princeton Architectural Press, Princeton, 1990, pp. 61–72 and Robert Somol, Dummy Text, or The Diagrammatic Basis of Contemporary Architecture, introduction to *Peter Eisenman. Diagram Diaries*, Thames & Hudson, London, 1999, pp. 7–25.

2 In fact it is possible to go further and argue that to the extent that programmatic criticality is denied then all that gets to be maintained are formal innovations.

3 P. Eisenman. Post/El Cards: A Reply to Jacques Derrida, *Assemblage*, No. 12, 1990, p. 16.

4 The development of this particular conception of negativity is detailed in Chapters 1 and 5. What is being staged here is part of the process by which finding an adequate terminology and conceptual scheme for developing architectural philosophy delimits the task at hand. While given architects are often concern to provide detailed theorizations of their own work, there is always the danger that such a theorization is unproductive and idiosyncratic and thus precludes the possibility of engaging with a more detailed range of architectural practices.

5 I have attempted to provide a more detailed interpretation of the Wexner Center in these terms in my Peter Eisenman and the Housing of Tradition, *Art, Mimesis and the Avant-Garde*, Routledge, London, 1991 and in Architeure et Contrainte, *Chimères*, No. 17, 1994, pp. 139–54.

6 P. Eisenman. To Adolf Loos and Bertolt Brecht, *Progressive Architecture*, No. 55, May 1974, p. 9.

7 J. Kipnis. P-tr's Progress in C. Davidson (ed.) *Eleven Authors in Search of a Building*, The Monaceli Press, New York, 1996.

CHAPTER 3

1 This text includes parts of an earlier study of Reiser and Umemoto's work published as Not to Shed Complexity in *Fisuras*, December 1995, No. 3, 1/4, pp. 46–57.

2 I have tried to analyse this structure of repetition in *The Plural Event*, Routledge, London, 1993.

3 Stan Allen has investigated this problem with great precision. Rather than merely positing an architecture of distance – understood as being either utopian on the one hand or the conflation of architecture and building on the other – he has called for what he describes as '*anexact* fit between event and structure'. See his Dazed and Confused, *Assemblage* 27 August 1995.

4 In a sense what is involved here concerns the new. How is the new in architecture to be understood? This is an extremely difficult question, This project

– writing about the projects of Reiser and Umemoto – can be seen as an attempt to engage with that question. It is thus that it would be possible to begin to respond to another important recent paper by Stan Allen. In From Object to Field in Peter Davidson and Donald L. Bates (eds) *Architecture After Geometry*. Academy Editions. London. 1997, while arguing for the viability of field conditions and signalling a return to a certain form of contextualism, he goes on to note that

> Field conditions treats constraints as opportunity and moves away from a Modernist ethic – and aesthetics of transgression. Working with and not against the site, something new is produced by registering the complexity of the given.
>
> (p. 24)

It is clear that for modernism, transgression and the new are productively interrelated. The difficulty with Allen's formulation is not just that the new is not defined – though in the end that will have to be a problem – it is that 'registering the complexity of the given' may count as precisely an act of transgression for urban theorists who maintain a fidelity to the simplicity of the grid and then define the deviant – perhaps even the delirious – as determined by it. Equally it will be a transgressive act if complexity means more than confusion. On a more theoretical level it can be argued that such a registration would have to be a transformation of the given. It is unclear that the given is given as complex either phenomenologically or for the most part theoretically. Returning to the given would therefore involve a transformation or a transgression. In the same way as it is difficult to shake the hold of modernism, it is equally as difficult to force a radical divide between transgression and a conception of the new that falls beyond the reach of a celebration of simple novelty.

5   This is a complex and demanding point. It means, in part, that the attribution of meaning, where that involves an equation of meaning and the symbolic, represses the presence of the object and thus represses the presence of the ontological. However, it is also the case that it is the actual presence of what was identified above as the object qua object that allows the symbolic to function in the first place. The project here involves trying to trace the consequences of recognizing their already present interarticulation.

6   This is, of course, the direct consequence of what has been called post-modern architecture.

7   Greg Lynn. The Renewed Novelty of Symmetry. *Assemblage*. 26 April 1995. p. 11.

8   It is precisely thus point that has been developed in relation to Eisenman's work in Chapter 2.

9   Even though it is a difficult point the relationship between the concept and the structure here should not be understood instrumentally. Indeed instrumentality will always demand a more exact relation than their project allows. Incomplete relations will demand a theorization that will have to operate

outside of a simple oscillation between the presence and absence of instru-mentality. The recognition of the state of affairs would serve to mediate the strictures advanced by Mark Wigely concerning a 'simplistic instrumental-ization of theory'. See his 'Story-Time' in *Assemblage* 27, August 1995.

10 I tried to develop this conception of the event in my *The Plural Event* Routledge. 1993. See in addition my Event, Time, Repetition in *Columbia Documents of Architecture and Theory*, Volume 4. 1995. The expression plural event is used in order to signal the presence of a founding irreducibility. However rather than the irreducible identifying either variety of diversity it has to be taken as ontologico-temporal in nature.

11 Stan Allen. *Assemblage*. op. cit. p. 54.

12 They have written extensively of their own use of the geodetic. The above quotation comes from the presentation of the Cardiff Bay project in *Assemblage*. No. 26. 1995. p. 36.

13 The range of issues involved in this project and the difficult and complex background to it, mean that it is only possible to take up certain aspects of it. I have emphasized issues to do with monumentality. I am not for a moment suggesting either that is all that there is to their project, or that there are not other aspects that may not have been directly addressed by their submission to the contest. What differentiates it from many others however is their acute recognition of some of the central issues involved.

CHAPTER 4

1 I have tried to develop this conception of ontology in *The Plural Event*, Routledge, London, 1993.

2 G. W. Leibniz, *Die philosphischen Schriften* (PS), ed. C. J. Gerhardt, Berlin, 1875–90, Band 6, p. 363.

3 PS Band 2, p. 450.

4 PS Band 5, p. 67, my emphasis.

5 Even though it can not be argued for here, this point forms a fundamental, though for the most part implicit premise of the entire argument; namely that time and existence are always interarticulated.

6 PS Band 6, p. 610. Inherent in this formulation is a birth that can only ever take place in its never fully taking place.

7 PS Band 6, p. 608.

8 PS Band 2, p. 170, my emphasis.

9 I have used the expression primordial presence as opposed to actual presence in order to distinguish between two modes of presence where the basis of the distinction is ontological. It must be added that this co-presence does not succumb to the logic of exclusion.

10 The term anoriginal is developed in the book cited in note 1. Its use involves an attempt to mark original difference, where that difference is ontological in nature and effective in outcome. It is a term whose stakes remain to be clarified.

11 PS Band 6, p. 609.
12 I. Kant, *The Critique of Pure Reason*, trans. N. Kemp Smith, Macmillan, London, 1983. All future references to this edition.
13 PS Band 2, p. 97, my emphasis.
14 The virtue of the concept of tradition is that it allows the question of history to be posed within philosophy as a philosophical question.
15 PS Band 6, p. 609.
16 I. Kant. *Logic*, trans. Robert S. Hartman and Wolfgang Schwarz. Dover, New York, 1974, p. 13.
17 *op. cit.*, p. 14.
18 See my 'Time and Interpretation in Heraclitus' in *Post-structuralist Classics*, Ed. A. Benjamin, Routledge, 1989.
19 An earlier version of this paper was given as a lecture to the Faculty of Architecture at Princeton University. I found the following discussion of great value and therefore wish to thank all those involved. I would also like to thank Peter Osborne and David Wood for their comments.

CHAPTER 5

1 M. Blanchot. Berlin, *Modern Language Notes*, 109, 1994, pp. 345–55.
2 This text is published in both French and English in *Yale French Studies*, No. 79, pp. 5–11.
3 Quotation is taken from the Loeb edition of *De architectura*, Cambridge, USA, 1953, p. 27. Translation by F. Granger.
4 While the complex interplay between the urban and the body cannot be considered here what is fundamental is to begin with the recognition that the way the interplay between architecture and the body is staged by Vitruvius, and it is a staging that is repeated throughout the history of architectural theory, demands a more sophisticated approach than one that operates only on the level of metaphor.
5 I have discussed the logic of this term in greater detail in Figuring self-identity: Blanchot's Bataille in J. Steyn (ed.) *Other than Identity*, Manchester University Press, 1997, pp. 9–32.
6 Blanchot, Enigma, p. 9.
7 G. Bataille. *Inner Experience*, p. 169, French, *Oeuvres Completes*, Tome 5, 422–3.
8 M. Heidegger. Building, Dwelling, Thinking in *Basic Writings*. Harper Collins, New York, 1993, German: Bauen, Wohnen, Denken in *Vortrage und Aufsatze*, Neske, Pfullingen, 1990.
9 I have discussed the role of a generative negativity in a number of recent essays. See in particular The Architecture of Hope, Daniel Libeskind's Jewish Museum in my *Present Hope*, Routledge, London, 1997 in addition to the more general treatment of this topic through this book.
10 M. Blanchot. *L'espace littéraire*, Gallimard, Paris, 1955, p. 136.
11 G. Bataille, OC, v: 156.

12 J. Derrida. Khora in *On the Name* (trans. I. McLeod) Stanford, USA, 1995, pp. 90–91. French: *Khora*, Editions Galilée, Paris, 1993, p.18.
13 In this regard see the detailed investigation of 'khora' in Chapter 1.
14 M. Blanchot, Berlin, p. 352.

<h2 style="text-align:center">CHAPTER 6</h2>

1 This is a point argued for with great clarity by Catherine Ingraham in *Architecture and the Burdens of Linearity*, Yale University Press, New Haven, 1998.
2 For further work in this area see my 'L'informe qui forme: Bataille, Deleuze and Architecture' in *D: Columbia Documents of Architecture and Theory*, Vol. 6, 1997, pp. 90–100.
3 Another history could be introduced at this point. With it the line would be directly incorporated into the history of geometry. It should not be thought however that the abstract line is necessarily distanced from the work of representation. For an important study showing how that relationship operates in the writings of Descartes see Claudia Brodsky Labour. *Lines of Thought*, Duke University Press, Durham, 1996. See in particular pp. 49–68.
4 The terms 'khora', 'informe' and 'crypt' demand there own detailed analysis. It would be an analysis that removed them from their initial context and began to investigate the potential that such terms had within the development of architectural theory. Part of this project appears in the discussion of Derrida and Bataille in Chapter 1. In other words, their interest would lie in the way they gave rise to an account of the development of form within architecture. The founding contexts for each of these terms is the following. J. Derrida. *Khora*, Galilee, Paris, 1993, G. Bataille, 'L'informe' in Tome I, p. 174, Gallimard, Paris 1987 and N. Abraham and M. Torok, L'écorce et le noyau in and *L'écorce et le Noyau*, pp. 56–93, Flammarion, Paris 1985.
5 It is this position that has been developed in Chapters 1, 2 and 3.
6 The references to Leibniz that occur here are taken up in much greater detail in *The Plural Event*. In regards to the architectural see the discussion of Leibniz in Chapter 4.

<h2 style="text-align:center">CHAPTER 7</h2>

1 Donna J. Harraway. *Simians, Cyborgs, and Women: The Reinvention of Nature*, Routledge, London, 1991.

<h2 style="text-align:center">CHAPTER 8</h2>

1 This paper was first given at a conference in Bucharest in 1997. The aim of the conference was draw together architects, social theorists and philosophers to discuss the implications of the architectural legacy in Bucharest and how to engage with it. The object of this paper was to set the scene from within

the history of philosophy for how destruction was to be understood and thus how the relationship between the new and destruction could be reformulated.

2 The reference to this distinction between ontology and semantics is an area of research that can only be addressed here in outline. It is pursued in greater detail in Chapter 1.

3 All references the Descartes are to R. Descartes, *Oeuvres Philosophiques* (ed.) F. Alquié, Tomes 1–111, Garnier, Paris, 1978.

CHAPTER 9

1 The ostensible concern of this paper is not to present an analysis of specific Holocaust memorials. My concern is more tentative. In the place of detail – recognizing, of course, its necessity – there is the attempt to take up and develop the philosophical basis for the evaluation and thus the judgement of Holocaust memorials. With the Holocaust the question of memory becomes urgent, contested and complex. My undertaking here has be to pursue, philosophically, the problem of memorialization, once the Holocaust becomes the occurrence that repositions any attempt to understand the activity of memory within modernity. A sustained investigation and recording of Holocaust memorial has been undertaken by James Young in *The Texture of Meaning: Holocaust Memorials and Meaning*, Yale University Press, New Haven, 1993. Whatever theoretical limits there may be to Young's work his book remains central to any investigation of this topic.

2 I have discussed this distinction in greater depth in my *Present Hope: Philosophy, Architecture, Judaism*, Routledge, London, 1997. See pp. 103–10.

3 The mistake made by Sartre in his *Réflexions sur la question juive* (Galimard, Paris, 1954) is that he conflates the identity of being a Jew and Jewish being at precisely this point. This is a conflation that marks any attempt to take up the presence of anti-semitism within any philosophy of totality. The philosophical challenge of racism is that the resources within both liberalism and humanism are inadequate to form the basis of any sustained response.

4 Even using the word Holocaust is problematic. There are a range of arguments concerning whether the word Shoah or Holocaust should be used. Here, however, that debate is not the issue. Nonetheless, it should still be recognized that using one term rather than another – and sometimes using the word Holocaust is already to yield to a certain constraint – is itself a move that allows for its own interpretation.

5 In this regard see Carl Schorske's magisterial study of the Ringstrasse, in his *Fin-De-Siècle Vienna*, Vintage Books, New York, 1981, pp. 24–116.

6 Michael North. The Public as Sculpture: From Heavenly City to Mass Ornament, *Critical Inquiry*, Vol. 16, Summer 1990, p. 878.

7 Andres Huyssen. Monumental Seduction, *New German Critique*, No. 69, 1996, p. 25.

8 For a more detailed discussion of the politics and practice of memory in the German context see Michael Geyer. The Politics of Memory in Contemporary

Germany. in Joan Copjec (ed.) *Radical Evil*, Verso, London, 1996.

9   It is not surprising in this regard that Holocaust memorial on supposedly 'neutral' ground poses fewer problems than the actual presence of the camps.

10 While this use of the term tradition may appear abstract and monolithic, it is more accurately an attempt explain the presence of the everyday in terms of the reiteration of already preconceived functions and therefore of already preconceived conceptions of the subject positions envisaged by those functions. Architectural form has for the most part to allow for the reiteration of that which is given to be repeated. That repetition – a determination in advance – is the work of tradition. In being its work it indicates the way in which repetition yields the site of intervention as well as the place of invention. Tradition as repetition always demands specificity. Specificity emerges, within this setting, once it becomes necessary to detail that activity of a given generic possibility within architecture.

ANNOTATED GUIDE TO FURTHER READING

1   The texts in order are *Architecture/Theory/Since 1968*, MIT Press, Cambridge, 1998. *The Oppositions Reader*, MIT Press, Cambridge, 1998. *Theorizing a New Agenda for Architecture: An Anthology of Architectural Theory for 1965–95*, Princeton Architecture Press, New York, 1996, and *Rethinking Architecture*, Routledge, London, 1998.

INDEX